The Unhindered Path

Ruminations on Shin Buddhism

THE UNHINDERED PATH

Ruminations on Shin Buddhism

John Paraskevopoulos

SOPHIA PERENNIS

First published in the USA
by Sophia Perennis
an imprint of Angelico Press
© John Paraskevopoulos 2016

Series editor: James R. Wetmore

For information, address:
4709 Briar Knoll Dr.
Kettering, OH 45429
www.@angelicopress.com
info@angelicopress.com

ISBN 978-1-62138-198-3 (pb)
ISBN 978-1-62138-199-0 (cloth)
ISBN 978-1-62138-200-3 (ebook)

Cover Art: Gabriela Stauffer
Cover Design: Laura Silvestri (AliaGrafica)

Respectfully, I say to all people who aspire to be born in the Pure Land: the ocean of the One Vehicle, the Universal Vow, has consummated the highest virtue which is unhindered, unbounded, supreme, profound, inexplicable, indescribable and inconceivable. . . . Since we accept and entrust ourselves to this teaching, for us it is the supreme dharma—the fundamental intent of the Buddha is nothing but freedom from birth-and-death for all, ourselves and others included.

Shinran

CONTENTS

ACKNOWLEDGMENTS

Sincere thanks are due to Mr Chris Morgan for his thoughtful and perspicacious comments which have assisted in enriching the text. I am also grateful to Mr Steve Bastasch, for the many helpful suggestions made to the manuscript, and to Mr David Quirke-Thornton for his very kind encouragement in support of this work. Finally, this book would not have been possible without the generous publication grant provided by the International Association of Buddhist Culture in Kyoto.

PREFACE

This book comprises a variety of works written over the past twenty years, including a selection of essays, sermons, pastoral advice, aphoristic reflections on a range of spiritual themes and other writings. While this compilation is broad-ranging in scope, it is hoped that there may be something of value or interest to most readers. To this end, every attempt has been made to offer a coherent and engaging vision of Shin Buddhism for modern audiences.

J. P.
Canberra
Festival of Flowers
April 2016

Buddhism poses the basic problem of life and the world. It delves deep into the interior of human existence and uncovers, from under the superficialities of pomp and pride, the presence of gloom where delusion and evil are rampant. Reason defies contradiction but the inner self cannot escape from being contradictory due to this spiritual darkness. We may aspire for a higher ideal, but we are fettered to saṃsāra with chains of causality. Buddhism calls into question the whole existence of a human being which reason fails to grasp, and provides a solution to it which no science or philosophy can ever hope to attain. Where reason ceases to function with its false discernments, the spiritual eye is opened to the shuddering reality of one's existence and to the all-embracing Mercy and transcendental Wisdom of Amida Buddha.

Kenju Masuyama

PART ONE

Reflections

Reflections

I

The tragic paradox of the human condition comes down to this: we are forever striving for permanence in the midst of what is transitory. We know full well that everything in this world comes to an end and yet this knowledge is never reflected in our aspirations—we always desperately seek to hold on to those things that we cherish, even while we watch them fade away before our very eyes.

II

Love, beauty, health, passion—what we treasure in life. Death, pain, disease, sorrow—what we cannot avoid in life. The constant effort to secure the former is more than matched by the endlessly frantic struggle to keep the latter at bay.

III

Concerning the goods of this world, no one can succeed in halting the onslaught of time and the instability that comes in its train. We appear to yearn for much more than we can ever grasp and our desires elude the capacity of life to satisfy them—like a broken dam where water seeps away through a crack, before the rain ever has a chance to fill it.

IV

What lies behind our experience of fear? It is the prospect of losing our well-being and loved ones, as well as the dread of certainty and meaning slipping through our fingers. When faced with a crisis, a child seeks assurances that everything will be well but, often, parents feel the need to conceal bitter truths. This concealment is the pall cast by reality over our poignant attempts to secure comfort, stability and happiness.

V

The many wounds we bear in our hearts are a sign of our radical incompleteness as human beings. Our capacity for woundedness is what it means to be vulnerable. While we fear being exposed in this way and do everything in our power to avoid it, vulnerability affords us a precious opportunity to see loss, death and suffering as portals to transcendence. It forces us to renounce our unsteady and agitated reliance on life's crippling limitations and to set a firm anchor in the deep, still waters of spiritual truth.

VI

The revulsion commonly expressed towards death reflects the horror felt by most people in the face of their impending oblivion. For many, this is naturally the greatest fear of all as it spells the end of everything known to us, without any prospect of recovery. What accounts for this rejection of death and its supposed finality? Is it just the sense of anguish in losing everything or are we conscious of an acute discrepancy—between the vitality of life and its opposite—that somehow does not seem quite right? In other words, perhaps the antipathy we feel in the face of our mortality is a sign that, in our heart of hearts, we know that we are meant for something more than mere annihilation; that our complete fulfillment as human beings is in an abiding and indissoluble life that surpasses all tribulation.

VII

The incongruity we often experience between desire and reality is the source of profound unease. It makes us feel that something is out of place in our lives. We cannot seem to reconcile our sublime quest for everything wonderful and joyous with the sobering realities of disappointment, disenchantment and despair. The impressive discoveries of science can never solve this problem for us nor can the powerful forces of commerce make this difficulty disappear. It is not simply a matter of accumulating sufficient facts or wealth. The solution must be, unquestionably, a spiritual one.

VIII

Life presents itself as a riddle, beckoning us to fathom its secrets and wonders. But it is a harsh and difficult riddle that does not yield its mysteries easily. In fact, its deepest disclosures are sometimes accompanied by experiences that burn. These can be purifying if we are open to the promptings of a wisdom that seeks to emancipate us from an inauthentic life.

IX

When we dream, we often enter a world of fugitive images and ambiguous emotions. It is hard to take stock of our bearings or to make sense of what we are undergoing. The experience can be unsettling as it leaves us unmoored and confused. It is only when we emerge from this obscure realm, following sleep, that we feel a sense of light and clarity. And yet, in how many ways does our waking world resemble our dreams? Perplexity, bafflement and anxiety appear to be common to both even though we are confident that our lives are definitely not dreams. Dreams may differ in the extent of their clarity and intensity, making some seem more real than others. Perhaps this life, too, is a dream of sorts—albeit a very vivid one—from which, when we die, we wake up. Seen from the aspect of that which is timeless, our tenuous and evanescent lives must indeed be so.

X

The fire of deep passion can be thrilling, intoxicating and unforgettable. It transports us to a point where we feel that there can be no higher purpose to our lives and that our deepest wishes for human fulfillment are perfectly realised. Of course passions can also be misdirected, causing great harm or they can be short-lived, despite their fervour, leading to disappointment and heart-ache. Is there a kind of delight that accompanies a passion that is both enduring and focused on the highest good? If so, might it be possible that such passion has its origin in something greater than self-interest or the ephemeral concerns of everyday life? We enjoy sunshine and all the blessings that come with it—fire, heat and light. While immersed in these, we may be apt to forget that their source is the sun, which is sustained by an inconceivable degree of energy and power. It is the same with passion. At its core lies a great fire of brilliant splendour and intense joy that survives all the fluctuations of love and hate, gain and loss, fear and desire, hope and failure. We feel its heat and we see its light but we must look beyond these in order to behold its full majesty.

XI

Undoubtedly, there is a vast shortfall between what we long for and the ability of life to meet our need for contentment. The conditions of this world are so precarious and fleeting that it is almost impossible to depend on anything with certainty. While this invariably causes us distress, we must get to the bottom of why this is so. In what lies our aversion to impermanence and imperfection? Why are we so grieved by the painful shortcomings of our frail existence? The fact is that who we really are cannot be identified with the fading phenomena in which we are steeped. This does not just include our material environment but also the personality we currently possess and everything it comprises: yearnings, disappointments, memories and desires. These too must pass with the dissolution of mind and body at the time of death. However, that part of us which laments our ephemeral life and seeks an existence without sorrow is not the ego that perishes. It is a higher self, in which we all share, that endures as an undying reality. If this was also subject to decay and destruction, like everything else, we would not in the least be concerned about our inevitable demise. This vague but deep intimation we have of immortality as our true nature allows us to see that death is not the end because we come to view it as having nothing to do with our real self.

XII

We are made for happiness. The core of our being demands it as an indispensable condition of our well-being. This fundamental requirement of our hearts tells us that there can be no substitute for it; nothing else can take its place. This is because its compelling hold over us lies in it being a natural extension of the joyous reality of Nirvāna which is true happiness, genuine liberation, source of all desire and our eternal destiny.

XIII

Buddhism speaks of an ultimate reality to which it gives many names. Some question its existence as they find it so difficult to fathom. Due to its inconceivable nature, the calculating self can never grasp it. And, yet, it is this reality that makes enlightenment possible and secures our final release from saṃsāra. It is also what guarantees the transformative power of Wisdom, which makes us see things as they truly are and gives us the confidence to abandon ourselves to the supreme Compassion.

XIV

The Dharma-Body is described in the sūtras as being the true and eternal reality behind all things. This makes it seem remote from us because everyday life is manifestly unsatisfactory and fleeting. It is difficult, therefore, to find a point of reference in our lives that can help us to accept and understand such a reality. It may, perhaps, be more helpful if we viewed it from another angle. We see shadows only because of the existence of light. Shadows are insubstantial and can only be perceived as such based on that which is unwavering or solid. Our lives are like shadows—their nebulous nature only becomes apparent to us because we discern a reality that, not only makes them possible, but frees us from their false enchantment by illuminating the truth of our existence. In this sense, the Dharma-Body is like the sun which sheds light on all beings and nurtures them to spiritual maturity.

XV

We live in a world where higher truths are reduced to lower ones, where everything is considered subjective and relative, and where the notion of anything being absolute is dismissed as naïve. However, those making such assertions consider them to be *true*; that is, impartially so and independently of what our personal feelings about them happen to be. And, yet, herein lies a profound contradiction. How can even the notion of truth be conceivable when the very thing that makes it possible, namely objective reality, is declared to be a fiction? The claim that 'all things are relative' must equally apply to that statement too thus invalidating its claim to be true. The only way around this impasse is to acknowledge that, as human beings capable of spiritual insight, we are endowed with the facility to see into the heart of things objectively. This fundamental intuition, shared by all the great Buddhist masters, makes us grasp the truth as something apart from what Shinran called the 'lies and gibberish' of our confounding everyday reality. It is the Dharma-Body that makes us realise this because it embodies the highest truth there is.

XVI

We usually take for granted the capacity, in our more lucid moments, to step outside ourselves; to catch a glimpse of who we are as if from the vantage point of an impartial witness. This is evident in such phenomena as self-awareness and the workings of our conscience. We can, and often do, pronounce judgements on our own thoughts and behaviour. Can this be the working of a higher self within us, one that is intimately imbued with the light of the Buddha? The boundless reach of this reality into our lives serves to hold a mirror to our everyday self. After all, how is it that we can be repelled by our ignorance, selfishness and cruelty if not for the presence of a wisdom in our hearts that, nevertheless, transcends this corrupted world? Otherwise, we would see nothing wrong in our misguided actions as long as they continue to serve our greed and self-interest.

XVII

The Dharma-Body, being ultimate, boundless and perfect reality, assumes form as that which is fragile, imperfect, dream-like and, therefore, full of affliction which we feel acutely as a result of this 'remoteness' from our source. Although our world of birth-and-death (samsāra) is manifested by the Dharma-Body in an impersonal manner, this does not mean that the reality behind this manifestation is also impersonal. Just as our bodies are host to countless involuntary processes that take place in accordance with physical laws, while having their foundation in a personal entity, so does the Dharma-Body give rise to innumerable expressions that are not willed or controllable but which, nevertheless, reflect its intelligence, beauty and love, as well as the complexity of the karmic forces that are inherent to it.

Our fleeting world, though arising naturally and spontaneously from the Dharma-Body, is also fuelled by the three 'poisons' of ignorance, anger and greed. And, yet, these two realms (the absolute and the relative) are inseparable. However, samsāra never has the final word seeing as the blazing rays of the midday sun will always dispel the heavy mists of the morning. The suffering and evils we endure in a fractured world such as this are thus unavoidable, being the price of impermanence which, though haunting us like a troubled dream, will be vanquished upon our arrival at the Other Shore.

XVIII

We cannot be rescued from a burning world through means of fire. Neither can we be spared the ravages of blind human passions via a remedy of even more anger, stupidity and avarice. If one is seeking an escape from suffering and discontent, from that which is disappointing and perishable, it stands to reason that one can only do so by relying on something dependable which is the opposite of the things that cause sorrow. Only the Dharma-Body as absolute and infinite reality, source of all joy and real happiness, can deliver us from what we come to see as a form of exile in this painful realm of samsāra.

XIX

The 'law' of karma is precisely that—an unyielding law that governs the spiritual, moral and physical realities of saṃsāra. As an intrinsic aspect of the Dharma-Body and expression of its inner workings, it cannot be divorced from the fundamental nature of the highest reality. The implacable operation of karma is embedded deep into the fabric of the universe but should not be confused with fatalism. While it determines (based on the quality of our previous existence) many aspects of the circumstances into which we are born, including our personal attributes and the environment in which find ourselves, it does not divest us of our free will, without which any meaningful spiritual life would be impossible. Nevertheless, the freedom of our otherwise 'karmic' self remains inscrutable, as it is essentially tied to the mystery of our indwelling Buddha-nature.

While the forces of karma will always remain largely impenetrable to us, we can remain confident that the principle of 'cause and effect', in keeping with the immutable dictates of this cosmic law, prevails without impediment. But this law, when adhered to with reverence and wisdom, will help us to overcome its bondage by grounding us in a state of tranquility where karma no longer prevails.

XX

It is very difficult to establish any kind of connection with a reality that is described as 'inconceivable' and 'formless'. Something so seemingly distant, even if it is considered the foundation of all existence, does not warm us or inspire the heart; it cannot provide much comfort or hope in the face of fear and despair. While some Buddhist sages, in very rare circumstances, have directly attained a liberating realisation of the Dharma-Body in states of deep meditation (an experience also known as Nirvāna), this is not a possibility open to most ordinary people living in the chaotic tumult of everyday life. However, because this reality is not indifferent towards us, it emerges from its 'isolation' to manifest—out of great compassion—forms that are intelligible to our understanding and to which we can respond with confidence and joy. These forms are *Amida* ('Buddha of Immeasurable Light and Life') and the *Pure Land* ('Realm of Utmost Bliss').

Reflections

XXI

Amida Buddha is arguably the most perfect personification of compassion in the history of religious experience—a conception of spiritual reality that is unsullied by anything petty, vindictive or threatening. Amida is pure mercy. The story of the Bodhisattva Dharmākara who, out of pity for all tormented sentient beings, sacrifices everything for their welfare and spiritual emancipation embodies this ideal in a very moving way. While having earned the merit to become a Buddha, he made solemn vows to renounce Nirvāna until he could emancipate all beings. A more sublime expression of limitless compassion can scarcely be conceived.

The sūtra tells us that, the vows having been fulfilled over an imponderable period of time, this bodhisattva became Amida Buddha who established a pure realm, free from pain and sorrow, for all who seek it. While not necessarily having taken place in ordinary human history, this story represents a spiritual fact of momentous significance which, though having occurred in a timeless dimension, is forever being renewed every time a person awakens to this powerful, transcendent event. According to tradition, our knowledge of this story is made possible by the historical Buddha, Shakyamuni, who imparts the teaching of Amida and his vows to us in this world, thereby revealing an intimate connection between the transcendent Buddha and the earthly one who manifests it.

XXII

The notion of judgement that we often see in other religious traditions is not found in Amida Buddha, who seeks only to save all beings without regard to their personal qualities or merit. Rather, the function of 'judging' is the sole preserve of karma which always remains strictly dispassionate in its operation. While unable to work outside its bounds, Amida Buddha nevertheless utilises this law in order to purify karma and overcome it; something that is done on our behalf—incapable, as we are, of doing it for ourselves.

We often hear that the compassion of Amida is unconditional. While it is true that the Buddha does not take into account our broken natures when seeking to deliver us from saṃsāra, neither is it the case that nothing is expected of us. The only requirement is a willingness, on our part, to seek Nirvāna and rid ourselves of our lamentable condition once and for all. This 'thirst' for emancipation creates the conditions for our receptivity to Amida's working once we let it into our hearts. And, yet, even this thirst is simply the permeation of the Buddha's fathomless desire to put an end to our unhappiness.

XXIII

It is said that the immeasurable light of Amida Buddha cannot be seen but, rather, is a light that enables us to see. It is what makes real vision possible by illuminating our lives and revealing the true nature of existence. This is deep perception that empowers us to apprehend reality through means bestowed by reality itself; any other kind of seeing involves deception, distortion and fragmentation.

The boundless life of Amida Buddha is not life as we know it for it transcends death, fear and pain. It is a forceful current that conveys a liberating exultation of which our earthly joys are but a dim reverberation and a faint echo.

XXIV

Is Amida Buddha a person? Insofar as we deeply value the notion of personhood, it is inconceivable that the Buddha is without this integral attribute. In other words, the highest reality can hardly be impersonal in the way that, say, a rock is so. Only a personal reality is capable of making vows to free sentient beings out of compassion for them. The very act of approaching suffering humanity, in the guise of Amida Buddha and the Pure Land, does not suggest an indifferent reality lacking in responsiveness or concern. So, clearly, Amida cannot be impersonal in this sense. Also, the fact that Pure Land devotees over the ages have enjoyed vivid and intimate encounters with the Buddha is further evidence of this. Unless we are prepared to dismiss their claims as mendacious or delusory, the reality of Amida Buddha as personal is incontrovertible. However, we must always bear in mind that this is a personality without limitations or imperfections and, thus, not merely human but one which we nevertheless assume upon our birth in the Pure Land.

XXV

In light of the previous reflection, it cannot be said that we abandon any sense of personality when we attain Nirvāna, even though we no longer possess the discrete individuality we have in this life (intimately bound up, as it is, with the minds and bodies we possess here). The particular form with which we have been endowed in this world is unique and unrepeatable, consistent with the cardinal doctrine of anattā. In the normal course of transmigration, we take on new forms (either in human or other realms) as influenced by our previous karma. But when the bonds of samsāra are finally broken for us, we receive the Buddha's sublime personality of fathomless wisdom and unbounded compassion. This is surely the basis of everything valuable and precious in human personalities so, in the end, nothing is ever lost; we simply return to our true self in the Pure Land, radiant with joy and transfigured by Amida's all-embracing light.

XXVI

In the traditional understanding according to the sūtras, the Pure Land is a realm created by Amida Buddha (in his previous bodhisattva form) as a result of the merit accrued in self-sacrificing practices over many aeons. It was commonly regarded as an ideal place, outside the negative influences of samsāra, where one could practise the Dharma under the direct guidance of the Buddha in preparation for the attainment of Nirvāna. It was also considered to lie in the 'West', the direction of the setting sun. The symbolism here is clear as the Pure Land is what awaits us at the 'setting' of our mortal lives. It is also depicted in the most extraordinary way as a place of endless wonders and astounding beauty, leading many to think of it as a kind of heaven. In Buddhism, however, even heavens (as hard as it may be to believe) are a part of samsāra and therefore life there is also ephemeral—although much longer and more delightful than ours—and its denizens are liable to eventually regress into less blissful realms if their sole intent is merely the pursuit of pleasure (however refined or spiritual), rather than enlightenment.

This is why, as Shinran realised, the Pure Land must be more than just somewhere we go to enjoy rapturous enchantments. When reflecting carefully on the descriptions contained in the sūtras, one notices that the gratification derived from the features of that realm are directly related to the Dharma and its blessings. It was then a short step to the full identification of the Pure Land with Nirvāna as our ultimate spiritual destination. In other words, the Pure Land is an upāya (or 'saving means') for conveying the inconceivable nature of enlightenment through forms that are immediately accessible and deeply attractive to us. This does not mean there are no posthumous states that do not resemble what we would consider a 'paradise'; just that they are far from comprising the Great Nirvāna which is the real goal to which the Buddha seeks to lead us.

Reflections

XXVII

It would appear that explicit or detailed accounts of Nirvāna have eluded its most illustrious exponents. Either it has been portrayed in largely negative terms in order to stress its ineffability (as we find in earlier Buddhism) or we see more affirmative praises of its nature—in terms of eternity, bliss, purity and true self—that we notice in the Mahāyāna. Explanations of Nirvāna as mere 'extinction', which one often encounters, are grossly inaccurate if what is being suggested is some kind of annihilation. Shakyamuni Buddha himself explicitly denounced such a view. What is actually being extinguished is the 'fire' of our perverted views, debilitating ignorance and destructive passions; in fact, all those burdensome impediments that separate us from the Dharma-Body and its limitless expanse of illumined awakening (which is the experience of Nirvāna). This is not something we come to acquire from 'without' but is the emergence of this reality (Buddha-nature) from our hidden depths where it has been buried over countless wayward rebirths. It is the shedding of everything that is alien to us, everything that hampers our complete fulfillment as spiritual beings. The happiness that accompanies this transformation is, as we are told by those who know, beyond words.

XXVIII

We often hear about 'birth in the Pure Land'. But *who* is born there and what kind of birth is it? In light of our earlier discussion, it ought to be clear that we do not go to the Pure Land as exactly the kind of beings that we are now. A transfiguration takes place whereby we discard those aspects of our ourselves that are false and perishable, thereby acquiring true immortality. It is not that our ordinary, everyday self becomes immortal—this is impossible (and hardly desirable)—but that what is eternal within us becomes liberated, so to speak, in order to rejoin its source, like a spark returning to its flame. So the real self is the Buddha dwelling in the seat of our true being. Does this then mean that we, as individuals, simply become lost in Nirvāna, indistinguishably merging and flowing into the one 'ocean' as we sometimes read in the sūtras? Not exactly. There is intense activity and diversity in Nirvāna, including the countless manifestations emerging from it in the form of bodhisattvas for example, but they are tightly bonded into one dynamic, but inseparable, whole. It is important to remember that because reality is non-dual, does not imply that everything in it is exactly the same or strictly identical. In an exalted realm such as this, we find ourselves at the very limits of what language can convey but we can surely sense, even here, that this 'oneness' does not preclude a rich plethora of spiritual dimensions and possibilities.

XXIX

The light that saturates the Pure Land of bliss is the same light that constitutes the reality of Nirvāna which encompasses all things. Amida Buddha, who is the personification of that light, is the very means by which are made to know and embrace it. In this sense, one can say that although this world is assuredly not the Pure Land, the presence of its light can be experienced here and now in the turmoil that is the 'impure land' of our everyday world. Once we have experienced this light for ourselves, there can no longer be cause to question the veracity of the countless sūtras and sages who have testified to the reality of Amida Buddha and his realm of unsurpassed happiness. This is no longer wishful thinking but the most compelling of proofs. Can you doubt the existence of the sun when you find yourself bathed in its light?

XXX

The 'Primal Vow' is a direct expression of the Buddha's nature. By virtue of his compassion, Amida desires the supreme good for each sentient being, which is none other than freedom from the distress of samsāra. This liberation leads to Nirvāna and the cessation of all suffering. In other words, the Buddha desires our enlightenment which effectively dispels our painful delusions and allows us to become one with the ultimate reality which is manifested as Amida's immeasurable light and life. Compassion, in its deepest sense, must mean this or it means nothing at all. The Primal Vow corresponds to our deepest desire for an existence without pain, suffering and unawareness; something which is not possible in our world of samsāra. The Buddha sees our plight and desires to deliver us from it. He does so in accordance with his wisdom which devises the most effective means of reaching out to us like a torch in the 'long night' of ignorance.

XXXI

Many of us live our lives in a kind of stupor. Although we often see life as unsatisfactory or even unbearable, we are not conscious that we are, in fact, drowning in the vast 'sea of birth-and-death'. It does not occur to us to either question why we find ourselves in such a state or to seek a way out of our predicament. Of course, we often think we can assuage our feelings of angst and unease by all manner of distractions but these remain 'samsaric' in nature and merely serve to divert us from our true quest—ultimately, they can only disappoint in view of the deceptive relief they provide. In seeking wealth, fame, honours and pleasures we think that we have found solutions to our deep-seated anxieties. These things are, indeed, desirable but they often leave us empty because they do not address the basic cause of this disquiet. They affirm and project our ego into the world. We want to be successful, admired and loved but we seek to do this through the accumulation of qualities that are fraudulent, either because we have no right to lay claim to them as our own or because they ultimately compound our unhappiness by separating us from our true aim in life.

XXXII

Sooner or later, we are likely to reach a spiritual impasse in our lives. When this happens, we have to come to terms with it and find a resolution or we will be left burying our heads in the sand, resigning ourselves to lives of weary and bitter mediocrity. Lives that shun this quest for truth seek to numb the pain by living in denial. This struggle is not easy and neither are the answers to our predicament. At the very moment when things appear to be utterly hopeless, as we vainly thrash about in the stormy ocean of saṃsāra, we may see a life-rope and instinctively reach out for it. This is not merely the result of any kind of rational or considered train of thought. There is no calculation here, no careful weighing up of self-interest; just an immediate and instinctual response of seeking deliverance from our existential pain. In the throes of our desperation, we recognise something we feel compelled to trust because there is nothing else.

This is more than just a leap of faith. It is a form of recognition, of knowledge, but one that cannot be purchased cheaply. It is only when we are at rock-bottom that such an awareness is able to dawn on us. It is only when our own resources are completely exhausted, when our conceit, arrogance and pride are thoroughly depleted, that we can extend our trusting hand to this saving light. It is only when we are stripped of every illusion and see ourselves as nothing, that our consciousness is able to recognise the Primal Vow and its full significance for the first time. When we find ourselves at this critical juncture, we can either fall prey to the abyss of doubt or raise our crestfallen gazes to the possibility of true and enduring emancipation.

XXXIII

Knowing that the Eternal Buddha actively pursues us, through every means, is deeply comforting. We no longer have to berate ourselves for our countless failures in following the Buddhist path, where we constantly stumble in our attempts to become better human beings. It is, of course, natural to strive to increase our wisdom and compassion but, in the end, these are not ours to create. Enlightenment can only come from Enlightenment itself and Buddhahood from the Buddha. We must, therefore, immerse ourselves in this reality and pay no heed to the barriers that seem to separate us from Nirvāna, for these will pass and—even now—can be eclipsed by the radiance of Amida's Eternal Light which surrounds us.

XXXIV

Faith in Shin Buddhism is a direct and lively realisation of Amida's compassion. It is a joyous insight into the nature of things and a constant source of trust, hope and awe, despite the many difficulties we face in this life. Because faith is grounded in Amida's working and its presence within us, it confers confidence in the truth of the Dharma and certainty regarding our eventual birth in the Pure Land. It is not possible to have this awareness with any measure of doubt mixed in because we do not generate faith within ourselves. The 'true heart and mind' that is *shinjin* arises in us through contact with Amida; it is the spiritual energy of the Buddha that courses through us, dispelling our inner chaos. In this way, we are granted immense gladness and deep contentment. Fear regarding our ultimate fate is banished and we respond in gratitude by calling Amida's name.

[handwritten margin note: doubt is not possible because shinjin is not generated by us]

XXXV

Considered in its most profound aspect, faith is wisdom (*prajñā*) given to us by Amida. It is not mere belief of the kind that can be readily contradicted by facts or which needs to await confirmation through subsequent direct experience. Given it is deeply rooted in the Buddha's awakening, faith is unassailable and indestructible, like a diamond. This is an organic development that takes place in each person as they hear the Dharma which allows the seed of faith to take root and flourish. In Shin Buddhism, faith is the sole cause of attaining Nirvāna because it is enlightened reality itself flowing through us and taking us back to itself. There is little we can do to bring this about except admit this benevolent force into our lives and allow it to do its work without hindrance.

XXXVI

To rely on 'Other-Power' is to acknowledge our very real limitations as human beings. It is to accept our nature as ordinary people who are often overwhelmed by the raging tempest of existence but who also willingly surrender ourselves to the compassion of Amida's Vow. This abandonment to something greater provides relief from our suffocating ego and allows us to behold an unending vista of wonder, peace and light that sustains us throughout life. The world is so framed by uncertainty and instability that it cannot offer this kind of comfort or assurance. And we should not think, for a moment, that this is some kind of easy way out for timid or weak-minded people who cannot face the realities of life. Reality is actually seen for what it is through such a vision because it is grounded in that which is time-less. This is the only solution to the problem of impermanence and the anxiety it induces in those who mistakenly harbour the belief that this world is all there is.

XXXVII

It is imprudent to think that Other-Power means 'no effort'. While there is nothing we can do to gain enlightenment through our feeble spiritual gropings, we nevertheless need to awaken to that which can enlighten us. This must involve engaging with the teaching and remaining receptive to its message. It also requires resisting our natural tendency to languor and sluggishness in our commitment. Overcoming this takes work as there is always a struggle involved in subduing our natural inclination to rely exclusively on our own initiative and strength. Of course, such attributes are perfectly laudable in managing the practicalities of our daily lives but, when it comes to entering the realm of Dharma, we need to suspend, as it were, our focus on self if we are ever to reach the spiritual haven to which only Other-Power can take us.

XXXVIII

The path of Other-Power is often described as 'easy' because Amida has accomplished all the necessary work for our liberation but it remains most difficult, all the same, because of our persistent refusal to recognise, and entrust ourselves to, the very means the Buddha has made available for our return to the Pure Land.

XXXIX

Saying the name of Amida Buddha (*nembutsu*) is an act of refuge in response to the call from the Other Shore. We say *Namo Amida Butsu*, not for any particular reason or with a view to gaining anything, but simply because we acknowledge that this call—and even our response to it—are Amida Buddha in action. It is the form taken by Amida in order to disclose his compassionate intention for us; this declaration is also an invitation to accept the Buddha's offer of salvation which, when we truly hear it, becomes irresistible to us. The joy and gratitude of our response to this call streams forth from our lips as the nembutsu.

XL

It has been recorded that, during the bloody Battle of the Somme in the First World War, the final words uttered by many soldiers, as they lay dying in the filthy and miserable muddy trenches, was 'Mother'. At the point of death, their hearts were filled with a powerful memory of deep love and tenderness—the only thing that mattered right then—which became expressed as the visceral utterance of that word. 'Mother' embodied all those overwhelming emotions that were surging within those young men in their last moments of life. All that love, devotion and longing suddenly became condensed into a form that needed to be articulated by the heart in the most extreme of situations, where it was the only solace available.

The nembutsu is also a cry from the depths—a potent condensation of the most profound things we are capable of feeling. At the same time, it is an exhortation from the Buddha urging us to abandon everything inessential in our lives so that we may return to an unfeigned existence.

XLI

Attaining shinjin does not depend on erasing our defects but it does presuppose a profound awareness of our imperfections while, simultaneously, permitting us to see that Amida Buddha accepts us regardless. Many people find this difficult to believe, because they feel that much more ought to be required, but that is precisely why this teaching is so compelling—and, in any case, how could one expect anything less of unfathomable compassion? In the end, it really is the only option for the spiritually destitute.

XLII

'Just as You Are'—one often hears that Amida Buddha, without question, embraces us with all our human blemishes. This is true but it does not give us licence to readily vent our worst vices and destructive urges. In keeping with the Buddha's ethical teaching, we should always aim to uphold its noble tenets at all times and to the best of our ability. This makes for a better and more humane world without any expectation of gaining 'merit'. Doing the right thing by others, showing care and concern for their well-being, not only reduces suffering in the world but shows gratitude to Amida Buddha who never rejects us even when we shamelessly revile the blessings that the Dharma offers. Like a loyal dog, abused by a senseless owner, who keeps on returning to its master without any trace of resentment in its heart, so does the Buddha always, and with infinite patience, stand by us to the very end; without judgement or condemnation.

XLIII

Why is it that simply having faith and saying the nembutsu is sufficient to deliver us from the dismal round of transmigration? How can something so seemingly 'slight' be potent enough to ensure the attainment of Nirvāna at the end of our lives? In fact, why—if he is so compassionate—does Amida Buddha not just save everyone regardless of their abilities? Two misconceptions are usually behind such questions. Firstly, it is crucial to see that the source of our spiritual emancipation is Amida, not anything we do or fail to do. Of course, we are urged to accept what the Buddha gives us but this is not ordinary self-willed action with a view to getting 'results'. Therefore, Amida Buddha is both the means and the end of spiritual practice. Secondly, Amida is not an omnipotent deity that acts in an unrestricted manner. The law of karma prevails even here which means that a karmic connection needs to be established with the Buddha in order for the Primal Vow to take effect in our lives. For us, this means to simply 'hear the Name', conceive joyful faith and aspire for birth in the Pure Land. Amida will take care of everything else.

XLIV

Shinran refused to condemn or criticise the views of other Buddhist sects. He readily acknowledged that they all comprise the many forms of medicine that the Buddha administered to the spiritually ailing. He taught the truth as he saw it and invited others to partake of this exalted vision without coercion or manipulation. There was no claim that his path was better—only that it was the one which was true to his condition, to his perception of the truth based on a direct experience of the Buddha's overwhelming compassion and to his own flawed human nature. In Shinran, we have an exceptional model of what it means to be a person of deep faith who is capable of remarkable tolerance with respect to the beliefs of others. In this current age of excessive, violent and unthinking spiritual rivalry, we would do well to heed his inspiring example.

XLV

Our modern world is not a place that is sympathetic to spiritual visions of life. It encourages a flat, grey and one-dimensional take on our existence. It tells us to abandon simplistic and childish beliefs in spiritual saviours and blissful realms. This, we are told, is nothing other than infantile escapism that fears dealing with the real problems of our world. Such unrelenting scepticism towards transcendent realities is what distinguishes our society from all that have gone before it. It has wreaked havoc with our inner lives and ultimate happiness by denying our capacity for abiding joy in things that this world cannot provide. Given the prevalence of such attitudes all around us, it is very difficult to break free from them and assert, with confidence, the vital importance of the truths that one finds enshrined in the Dharma. Assert them we must, however, or we risk forgetting the reason as to why we are alive and find ourselves here.

XLVI

The power possessed by beauty in this world is such as to transfigure how we think and feel. It delights us to the core of our being and gives a compelling intimation of something greater in our lives that can leave us deeply moved and humbled. Beauty is like the bliss of Nirvāna descending onto our parched world, like soothing rain, taking the form of the countless things that move us and make us cry out in exaltation. When we hear about the millions of devotees, over the ages, who aspired to return to the Pure Land, it is clear that they must also have been pining for their return to the fount of all beauty.

XLVII

When we feel joy, we experience what it means to be authentically human. Of course, our worldly joys come and go, and this is indeed a profound source of sorrow for us. And yet there are some joys that abide under the surface of ordinary life; joys that endure the blows of everyday existence. When reading the sūtras, one often comes across something called *kangi*. It is a type of joy that entails being gladdened both in one's body (*kan*) and one's heart (*gi*). Shinran says that its meaning is 'to rejoice beforehand at being assured of attaining what one shall attain'; in other words, *kangi* is rooted in the future prospect of birth in the Pure Land, but is something which makes us jubilant now. We see then that this joy cannot be unsettled by the trials and disappointments of life because it does not depend on the mutable conditions of the world. The felicity of such a state is inviolable.

XLVIII

The message of Shin Buddhism, in essence, is this: At the heart of life is a radiant, blissful reality that is compassionate and eternal. It is deeply implicated in the world of birth-and-death from which it forever seeks to deliver us. It does so because we belong to that reality, even though we often fail to see this. And all it asks of us is to consent to have its liberating power dispel our spiritual desolation so that we may rejoice in knowing who we really are and where we are going.

Yet how can we purify ourselves spiritually by our own individual or social efforts? This is manifestly impossible, as anyone knows who has tried, since it is the ego that, by its own self-will and effort, undertakes the task. And so all its endeavours, no matter how altruistic and well-intentioned, must inevitably end in failure because of its heavy load of karmic residues: the past thoughts, words and deeds of ourselves and all our ancestors, which contaminate with egoism everything that we think, say and do. Only the Awakening of Faith, that radical change of heart caused by the gratuitous transference of the boundless merit of Amida Buddha from his supra-human store, can now purify us spiritually. Individual unselfishness or social morality, economic and political panaceas, cannot accomplish this alone. Only the death of the ego in utter selflessness, that turning about in the deepest seat of conscious being—the only miracle recognised by the Buddha—can transfigure us and our world with wonder, like the silent benediction of snow.

Harold Stewart

PART TWO

Sermons

The following excerpts are from sermons delivered at the Hongwanji Buddhist Mission of Australia in Sydney during the period 1995–2015.

Nirvāna

Nirvāna is, doubtless, the most important concept in Buddhism. Of course, it is more than just a concept—it is a living reality that pervades everything. Although we often speak about it as something that we may attain in the future, even after death, it is important to remember that its presence is manifested to us every day in ways to which we are often oblivious.

The literal meaning of the word *Nirvāna* is 'blown out' or 'extinguished' as in the quenching of flames. In his famous *Fire Sermon*, the Buddha spoke of people 'burning' with the 'fires' of attachment, hatred and delusion. The attainment of Nirvāna, therefore, represents the dousing of the existential conflagrations that are the cause of our suffering in this world and unfavourable rebirth in the next.

Nirvāna is also the reality to which the Buddha attained in his Enlightenment. This was described by the Buddha as a realm of bliss, purity and peace—the complete fulfillment of all our deepest hopes and aspirations. In the Mahāyāna sūtras, it is taught that Nirvāna, also known as the Buddha-nature in its indwelling aspect, comprises our true self to which we awaken when our dark minds are vanquished.

In Shin Buddhism, Nirvāna is presented in more concrete terms as the 'Pure Land' of utmost bliss and happiness—a realm into which we are 'born' after we die. This is another way of referring to the attainment of Enlightenment. The Pure Land tradition also considers Amida Buddha as the dynamic and personal dimension of Nirvāna, reflecting its compassionate aspect in a form to which we can respond with entrusting hearts. The awakening of *shinjin*, which is, in fact, the arising of Amida Buddha as a spiritual force within our own minds, is also the activity of Nirvāna itself working towards making itself known to all sentient beings and carrying them to its liberating shores.

It is important, then, not to see Nirvāna as a static or abstract reality that is cold and remote. It is the very essence of life, love and beauty which reaches out to all of us in the irresistible forms of Amida Buddha and the Pure Land.

Faith

There appears to be a renewed debate brewing in certain circles over the appropriateness of using the English word 'faith' to describe the paramount experience in Shin Buddhism, often referred to as *shinjin* in Japanese. The dispute centers on whether using 'faith' misrepresents the experience in question owing to the baggage with which this term is invested by the Christian tradition. On the other hand, some commentators are loath to rely on a technical Japanese word to describe such an important realisation given its lack of natural resonance for English speakers. Clearly, there is some merit in both positions and it seems important, therefore, that any resolution of the problem attempts to do justice to both concerns.

Firstly, it is worthwhile to point out that the word 'faith' has a much broader meaning than that which is usually ascribed to it in conventional theological discourse in the West. It has its etymological roots in the Latin word for 'trust'—not a blind trust, of course, but a confidence based on an apprehension of the truth. In this respect, it is opposed to doubt in that it presupposes a strong conviction of certainty unlike 'belief', with which it is often confused and which sometimes has an aspect of wishful thinking to it. Faith, therefore, is grounded in a feeling of certainty and not in the projection of arbitrary or capricious emotions.

This absence of doubt is not generated by purely logical considerations (whence the superficial criticisms it often attracts by narrow-minded rationalists) but by spiritual intuition or 'cardiac intelligence'—both immediate and compelling—which is known by Buddhists as *prajñā*. This is none other than the Buddha's wisdom as imparted to us and it is, precisely, that which gives faith its power and conviction. It is a knowledge that transcends limited human reasoning and provides a beacon of illumination and joy in our otherwise dim world of ignorance (*avidyā*). Faith, therefore, far from being a belief in things that cannot be proven is, on the contrary, the very foundation for any and, indeed, all certainties that we are able to apprehend. It is the very touchstone that makes truth possible at all—not because of any merit or wisdom on our part but because its source is the Buddha of Infinite Wisdom. Faith is this very wisdom as it is manifested through our hearts and minds.

We can say then that, although *shinjin* is a traditional term that is rightly used in many contexts when discussing the Shin experience, it can also be said to lack organic roots in our own culture and language which call for a more familiar and natural term to describe something so fundamental. The proper response to the complaint that 'faith', as ordinarily used, fails to do justice to this experience is not to abandon the term altogether but to rehabilitate it to its original and proper meaning. And this requires that we make all necessary efforts to dispel any misconceptions and to explain—responsibly and accurately—the full import of the 'Other Power' faith to those who seek spiritual sanctuary in Amida Buddha.

Refuge

During his spiritual struggles, Shinran became acutely aware of the hazard posed for each individual by the unconstrained ego. In his *Hymns of the Dharma-Ages*, he writes:

> Ignorance and blind passions abound,
> Pervading everywhere like innumerable particles of dust;
> Desire and hatred arising out of conflict and accord
> Are like high peaks and mountain ridges.

> Sentient beings' wrong views grow rampant,
> Becoming like thickets and forests, brambles and thorns;
> Filled with suspicion, they slander those who follow the
> nembutsu,
> While the use of violence and the poison of anger spread
> widely.

We need not look very far in our world to see countless examples of humanity's ever-darkening descent into madness, cruelty, greed and despair. We are also commonly confronted by the depths of degradation to which our lives can sink when they remain unilluminated by the wisdom and compassion of the Buddha. When confronted by so much vexation, fear and uncertainty, one may well ask: 'Can I be certain of anything in the world? On what can one truly depend in this life of endless disappointments?'

Shinran's answer was to urge people to seek refuge in Amida, the Buddha of Immeasurable Light, in whom lasting deliverance is to be found. In the *Hymns of the Pure Land*, he says:

> The light of purity is without compare.
> When a person encounters this light
> All bonds of karma fall away;
> So take refuge in Amida, the ultimate shelter.
> The radiance of enlightenment, in its brilliance, transcends
> all limits;
> Thus Amida is called 'Buddha of the Light of Purity'.
> Once illumined by this light,
> We are free of karmic defilements and attain emancipation.

Being none other than Nirvāna, the Buddha's realm is one of peace and unutterable happiness. It transcends this world of grief yet permeates it limitlessly. All we need do is to open our hearts to the ever-present reality of Amida and accept the freedom he offers from the nightmares created by our ego-centric drives and appetites which are never satisfied, however hard we may try to do so. Shinran's message may seem stern and uncompromising but he is merely describing the world as he sees it; with wisdom and full clarity. Ultimately, however, his message is one of great joy—a joy that accompanies the certain knowledge that the Buddha, in his inconceivable compassion, assures us of his illumination and grace throughout our voyage into eternity.

Scepticism

Our contemporary age seems unparalleled in its sceptical attitude regarding spiritual matters. It is as if modern man now considers himself fully 'adult' and therefore not in need of what is viewed as the emotional crutch of religion. In fact, it is often an acute source of embarrassment to many people to have to admit, among their peers, that they subscribe to any kind of religious faith for fear of scorn or ridicule. We pride ourselves in having outgrown the superstitions of our fore-fathers and in cultivating a more 'mature' outlook that is satisfied with the fruits of scientific thought and the rich bounty it has given to our lives. No more, it seems, of the benighted delusions of the past with their false attachment to an outmoded world-view which has, it is claimed, retarded the civilised progress of people for thousands of years by its preference for another, higher, world to this mundane one. We are told, by people who know everything and believe in nothing, that all is well without having to think about anything other than what lies directly in front of our noses.

Although this outlook still dominates today, fissures have already begun to appear in the seemingly impregnable fortress of the modern world with its values of materialism, scientism and reductionism. However, who would argue that people today are necessarily happier or more fulfilled? What price has been paid in abandoning the spiritual certainties which have marked the countless lives of those in traditional societies throughout the ages? We see before us a pallid world stripped of all its mystery and wonder—a vale of misery which is perpetuated by false promises but where happiness is sought in all the wrong places and where real knowledge is simply equated with cleverness and cunning.

A fundamental aspect of the Buddha's teaching was the impermanent and unsatisfactory nature of human life. This much should surely be obvious to any thinking and sensitive human being. But this was not all the Buddha taught lest his message be seen as one of unmitigated despair. However, many people today have simply resigned themselves to the reality that this is all that life is or has to offer and that we simply have to struggle to make the best of a bad situation. This is often done by distracting ourselves with the glittering fruits of modern civilisation such as the captivating new advances in technology. These, while purporting to increase our comfort and leisure time, only serve to heighten anxiety by their very banality and inability to truly satisfy our deepest need. What is this need? The Buddha's answer to this question was: 'Unceasing Light and Illimitable Life'.

In speaking of such things, the Buddha was not merely indulging in unattainable abstractions. He was trying to open our jaded eyes to the true nature of things in contrast to the dream-like world we inhabit in our everyday lives; lives often marked by misfortune, frustration and futility. The Buddha needed to call a 'spade a spade' when talking about life in order to shake us out of our spiritual listlessness and point the way to genuine human fulfillment. 'Unceasing Light and Illimitable Life' refer to the highest wisdom and compassion which characterise the transcendent nature of the Buddha's reality which is also known as *Nirvāna*—the state of perfect enlightenment and blessedness. To many people, such talk must seem like speculative nonsense without any bearing on the stern realities of the 'real' world. However, the Buddha extended an invitation to all people, over two and a half thousand years ago, that still remains relevant today. He invites us to follow a path, to undertake a journey—often difficult but deeply rewarding—that will eventually see us through our trials and suffering. He asks us to do so without biased preconceptions and in a spirit of trust and confidence. A path that has clearly afforded millions of people such hope, consolation and spiritual prosperity surely deserves to be tried and tested rather than dismissed out of hand. Do we fear that there may be more to life than our bleak resignations? It is never too late to take our first, albeit tentative, steps towards the Buddha's realm of light. Nobody is excluded from his invitation to a life that is enriched by the compassion that dwells in the very heart of reality itself and which imparts its nourishing joy to all who entrust themselves to its wisdom.

Once our eyes have been opened in this way, there can be no more room for indecisiveness or despondency, for this very awakening is true knowledge itself that confers a certainty and happiness which cannot be shaken by the clamour of this world.

Imperturbability

There is an expectation, among many people, that the purpose of any religious teaching is to promote spiritual well-being and endow us with qualities such as serenity, happiness and strength. It is often assumed that this is simply done by a feat of 'positive thinking', i.e., the elimination of all negative elements in one's nature and outlook. By just purging oneself of these hindrances, it is expected that one can attain a state of imperturbability (similar to the *ataraxia* of the ancient Greeks)—a tranquil conquest of the ordinary human passions that debilitate us.

Unfortunately, the way in which such teachings are often presented leads to unrealistic expectations which can be psychologically harmful. In striving to transcend the infirmities of our mortal condition, one often forgets to be altogether human, with all the frailties that this entails. In other words, the self-conscious pursuit of spiritual perfection almost invariably leads to a disfigurement of our real nature and to an act of violence done to our psyche. Why should this be so? The human condition is deeply ambiguous and full of terrible paradoxes that cannot be simply charmed away by a formulaic course in meditation or the undertaking of conventional good deeds. To live authentically means to be completely aware of this condition; both the majestic joyful peaks and the dark abysses that can wreak so much torment in our lives. Neither is a genuine spiritual path about improving our self-esteem. Sometimes the honest pursuit of enlightenment requires us to confront some appalling truths about ourselves—a confrontation that is an indispensable prerequisite for genuine liberation.

Shinran, pre-eminently among the great spiritual teachers of the world, was painfully aware of the difficulty in following a spiritual path without hypocrisy and self-deception. This led him to the conclusion (formed not without some courage) that perfection, in the traditional Buddhist sense, could not be attained while we remain fully human; that is, finite, conditioned and flawed. Accordingly, while possessing minds likened to 'snakes and scorpions', Shinran believed that we cannot rely or place any confidence in such an inherently unstable entity as our ordinary self in order to resolve the acute existential crisis in which we are immersed. All this must sound rather pessimistic but, in truth, it is the beginning of a realisation that can bring the greatest spiritual relief.

In order to fully appreciate Shinran's thinking, one must accept, or at least be open to, the reality of the Buddha—more precisely, the Buddha of 'Immeasurable Light' (*Amida*). Many today find it difficult to accept such a reality but this is more often the result of unquestioning prejudice rather than any reservations based on an open and impartial exploration of the spiritual life.

Through the spiritual practice of the *nembutsu* (the invocation of Amida's name—*Namo Amida Butsu*) the radiant world of the Buddha is opened up for ordinary people who are then left with no option but to completely entrust themselves to its beneficent working. Such an attitude of faith and entrusting is known as *shinjin* which is really the dawning of Amida's light within us. It is through our awakening to this light, that we can truly see ourselves as we really are—and thus be freed from the fetters that bind us to a life of needless suffering. In doing so, we allow the Buddha's life to transform our own, thus bringing us to the peaceful threshold of Nirvāna when we eventually abandon our human form at the time of death. But even now, the life of shinjin is a source of constant consolation for, although it shows us a mirror to our real self and its endless deceptions, at the same time it illuminates the path to freedom from such bondage. In this way, we can attain true selfhood through our natural affinity with Amida Buddha and the boundless, enlightened life with which he enfolds our brittle existence.

Vulnerability

In modern society, people often go to great pains to avoid appearing vulnerable. Vulnerability is commonly seen as a weakness which betrays our innermost frailties and exposes the fears we are reluctant to show the world. This can sometimes lead to us assuming a false sense of control over our lives and an unwillingness to be candid with our emotions. The fear of becoming hurt or wounded, in our relationships with other people or in our dealings with the world, serves to undermine our capacity for intimacy and self-knowledge. All these tendencies, which are quite common, are capable of causing much distress and suffering in our lives. They can stunt our inner growth and prevent us from becoming fully human—as precarious as that can be.

We often feel that there are no resources to draw upon in coping with life except our own sense of right and wrong, and that this justifies us in shutting out the world and blunting our receptivity to its vital experiences. If all we can rely on is our view of how things appear to us, we may very well be able to protect ourselves, to some degree, from being overwhelmed by those realities that can hurt us. In doing so, however, we may also be depriving ourselves of other perspectives which can help us to overcome some of the difficulties from which we seek to flee.

Shakyamuni Buddha taught that the root of much of our suffering can be found within us; that it is our own prejudices and false impressions that provide the fuel for sustaining our endless anxieties. This, in turn, perpetuates our belief in a permanent and stable self that is but a chimera which life's troublesome experiences soon expose. By fuelling this sense of a 'self' that is separate from others and disconnected from the surrounding world, we soon begin to form a hardened shell around us which lets nothing in and which slowly, but surely, leads to spiritual atrophy through lack of proper nourishment.

By encountering the Buddha's Light, we naturally feel compelled to abandon ourselves to it and come to resist our ingrained tendency to conceal our innermost fears and anxieties, for we willingly choose to surrender these as well. When we genuinely experience the immense compassion of the Buddha, we cannot but joyfully abandon the shackles with which we have allowed ourselves to be bound. No longer entrusting ourselves to our myopic views, we are free to express our full individuality without fear of being hurt or judged harshly by others. We learn to accept ourselves, with all our imperfections, because we are accepted by the source of life itself which does not discriminate between the good and the bad, the young and old or man and woman.

Accordingly, we learn to become 'our foolish selves' as the Pure Land master Hōnen once said. We cease trying to do violence to ourselves by abandoning all attempts at conforming to a false image of who we are—an image created by self-centred obsessions which imprison us and cut us off from everything that is true and real. Ultimately, surrender is the key for it relieves us of our karmic burdens and allows us to become authentic individuals untrammeled by the need to pretend to be better, or even other, than what we really are.

The Self

A long-standing traditional Buddhist concern has been with the concept of the 'self' (*attā*). One often hears that Buddhism is concerned with overcoming the ego-centric perspective in one's outlook on life. Indeed, this is seen as the root cause of much of the suffering and anxiety that afflicts all people. Why is it that our conventional belief in a self should be the occasion for so many difficulties in our lives? Can we possibly achieve an ego-less state of awareness? What are we left with in the absence of any kind of self?

The Buddhist tradition teaches that what we consider our everyday self comprises a collection or bundle (*skandhas*, literally 'heaps') of personal constituents, such as form, perception, feeling, volition and consciousness, which are fleeting and conditioned. Indeed, they are constantly changing throughout our lives and eventually dissipate at the time of death. Thus Buddhism denies that this 'person' or 'individual', to which we seem so inordinately attached, is in any way a permanent entity. Accordingly, it endures only for as long our lives do. However, the karma generated by our actions, which are informed by the operation of the *skandhas*, is capable of generating another individual (not necessarily in human form) subsequent to the dissolution of the physical and mental elements of our current existence. In other words, although our current personality does not survive, it nevertheless forms the seed for a future existence based on unresolved karmic tendencies and dispositions that must continue to play themselves out. Therefore, what survives in each succession of rebirths is not our self, or the individuality that we comprehend in this life, but the karmic 'current' that runs through them all like a thread of necessity fuelled by an endless chain of cause and effect.

In Buddhism, this outcome is considered to be highly undesirable as it involves further suffering in the arena of birth-and-death or *samsāra*. This realm is one of pain and delusion, the complete antithesis of the enlightened state which the Buddha attained in his great awakening under the Bodhi tree. It is precisely to extricate us from this that the Buddha taught his message for forty-five years. He did so by exhorting us to encounter that which transcends samsāra and alone is capable of securing our release from the misery of constant rebirths. This reality has many names but the most familiar of them is *Nirvāna*. The only true peace of mind that is possible in our fragile human state is to become awakened to this reality. It is only when we come to this awareness that we can properly be said to have fulfilled the meaning of our existence and thereby put an end to the karma that perpetuates future rebirths. As all such existences are finite and marked by imperfection, there can never be any true resting place for us in samsāra.

The Pure Land tradition of Buddhism has been very sensitive to the existential anxieties we face in trying to free ourselves from the chains of despair and meaninglessness that we constantly face in our transitory lives. While recognising the inexhaustible reality of Nirvāna as our ultimate resort, it is also realistic about the innumerable impediments we face as ordinary people in trying to find genuine spiritual alleviation from the incessant demands of our everyday self and its endless cravings. Indeed, the Pure Land faith denies the possibility that we can ever completely rid ourselves of our ego-centred existence, so long as we remain ordinary people. In fact, to be human is, precisely, to be subject to constant frustrations and disorder. This highly unsatisfactory state of affairs is the central insight of the Buddha's teaching on *dukkha*. So what is to be done? Is there a way out of this seemingly hopeless morass?

The solution, while appearing to be deceptively simple, is, in fact, among the most difficult accomplishments but not necessarily for the reasons that one might expect. We must remember that the very thing to which we are most attached, namely our self, is the very thing we must surrender. Of course, we can only yield to something real, otherwise such an act would be pointless. Amida Buddha, as the personal dimension of Nirvāna, is therefore not some kind of lifeless force but a vibrant and compassionate influence in our lives. There is no escaping its presence even though we may remain oblivious to it. Nevertheless, it is able to summon us from the hidden depths of reality, if we could but only lend our ears to this call.

Practice

Extremely difficult is it to put an end to our evil nature;
The mind is like snakes and scorpions.
Our performance of good acts is also poisoned;
Hence, it is called 'false and empty practice'.

The above verse from Shinran addresses itself to an important reality faced by many who aim to follow the Buddhist path; namely, the sense that the integrity of our practices is vitiated by an awareness that the spiritual life is often beset by egoism, hypocrisy and failure. Despite our most sincere and ardent endeavours, we are confronted with the realisation that we are no better than we were before and certainly no closer to the expected goal of enlightenment. One does not wish to over-generalise and discount the exceptions to this phenomenon but exceptions they certainly are. For most ordinary people, there comes a time when a stalemate is reached—if they have been practicing Buddhism in earnest—with the awareness that however hard one may meditate, practise 'good deeds' or cultivate virtue, one is not necessarily able to divest oneself of the chronic imperfections that plague us as human beings. In fact, it is often through these resolute efforts that such an awareness is deeply impressed upon us for the first time. For many, this can be an utterly crushing experience leading to terrible despair. Such an experience, regrettably, also leads many people to abandon Buddhism altogether because of a feeling that one is somehow a fraud in not being able to measure up to the exacting standards laid down by the Buddha for attaining enlightenment and overcoming the mind's disarray.

It is quite true that Buddhism, for the most part, appears to be very demanding in the perfection it expects of those who would follow the path to awakening. At the time the Buddha was alive, and under his immediate influence, it certainly appears as if many individuals were able to attain enlightenment in their very lifetime. There are many episodes recorded in the sūtras of the Buddha helping people to a deeper realisation of the Dharma through simple acts such as an exchange of a few words, a smile or the holding up of a flower with nothing needing to be said. The personal presence of the Buddha himself must have been powerful and unforgettable for those fortunate enough to belong to his order or to have crossed his path. Such good fortune must also have made possible the almost miraculous transformations in people that one reads about in the scriptures.

However, the Buddha himself did prophesy that this would not always be the case and that, with the passage of time following his entry into Nirvāna at death, the capacity of individuals with respect to practicing the dharma would degenerate to the point that no one would be able to attain enlightenment through traditional practices and observances. In fact, he lamented that during the period known as the 'Decadent Age of the Dharma' (in which we currently find ourselves) the Buddha's teaching would exist more in the letter than in the spirit. Many consider this explanation to be just an excessively pessimistic allegory; however, it is difficult to deny that we are living in an age where spiritual life is undergoing a gradual debasement and that one is hard-pressed to find, in the world today, any widespread prevalence of genuinely enlightened people of the stature of the Buddha himself or even of his greatest disciples. Of course, there is no shortage of spiritual leaders today making extraordinary claims for themselves but they are quickly discovered to be dangerous charlatans who do much more harm than good—'ye shall know them by their fruits'.

Does this mean that the Dharma is dead and without meaning in the modern world? Should Buddhism just become an object of quaint curiosity, merely a subject for academic study without any personal engagement in its vital teachings? Assuredly not. In the thirteenth century, Shinran challenged us to take a very hard look at ourselves and advocated a ruthlessly honest approach in our understanding of the world. He also asked us to take a hard look at what we mean by 'practice'.

Like all Buddhists of his time, Shinran stressed that practice was essential if one was to secure the primary objective of the Buddhist path—the attainment of Nirvāna. But how could he do this when he was such a vociferous critic of human nature, his own included, and when he despaired of the efficacy of individual practice in attaining such a lofty goal?

The answer to this question, while implicit in the doctrines of the Pure Land tradition, only became fully explicit in the insights provided by Shinran to this problem. In effect, he reversed the traditional concept of *ekō*, whereby one transfers to others the merit accrued in spiritual practice, to state that it is ultimate reality itself, or Suchness (*tathatā*) embodied as the Buddha of Immeasurable Light (*Amitābha*), that 'practises' on our behalf. In other words, the reality which we seek to attain in the state of Nirvāna has to act as the very catalyst that makes such an attainment possible in the first place. How else can we, as constricted beings relying on our paltry resources, be capable of scaling the heights of the Infinite without access to the power inherent in the Infinite itself? If we do not do this, what meaning can merely human practice have?

The Chinese master, Shan-tao, employs the powerful image of people grasping at sundry practices as if sweeping fire off their heads but getting nowhere in the process. Practice then just becomes another, albeit much more subtle, vehicle for manifesting our blind passions and selfish desires (minds like 'snakes and scorpions') rather than for purifying all traces of our ego-attachment. How is it possible to transcend that which is imperfect and limited through means that are exactly the same? It turns out, after all, that the very disease we are trying to cure is the subject of a treatment that is similarly infected.

This profound contradiction struck Shinran deeply. Accordingly, the only solution, as he saw it, had to be a radical one: complete abandonment of all self-willed attempts to attain enlightenment through purifying practices, coupled with a total surrender to the Buddha's working to liberate all sentient beings. Nothing else is required. This may strike some as absurdly simple. Others may question the effectiveness of such 'non-practice'. However, when you consider that the only reality that truly exists is the Buddha's Boundless Life, why not rely on it to secure your safe passage to the Land of Light that is Nirvāna? Why waste a precious lifetime in fruitless and painful struggle, trying to attain the very thing that is being offered to you without conditions?

The bottom line in any meaningful and valuable spiritual path is its capacity to furnish genuine relief from the suffering and existential travail that mark life in this world of 'endurance' (*saha*). In making the 'self' the object, rather than the subject, of practice, the Pure Land way does precisely that. The Buddha's 'practice' in freeing us is manifested as our gradual but spontaneous letting go of the very things that bind us to our doubts and perplexities. Our objective then is to allow the Buddha to do his work—unimpeded and without resistance. If we are, indeed, capable of any practice at all, then let it be this.

Deep Mind

'Deep mind' is the deeply entrusting mind. There are two aspects. One is to believe deeply and decidedly that you are a foolish being of karmic evil caught in birth-and-death, ever sinking and ever wandering in transmigration from innumerable aeons in the past, with never a condition that would lead to emancipation. The second is to believe, deeply and decidedly, that Amida Buddha grasps sentient beings and that, allowing yourself to be carried by the power of the Vow without any doubt or apprehension, you will attain birth in the Pure Land.

The above quote from Shan-tao sets the scene for a few observations on the nature of religious experience in Shin Buddhism. It is common to find, not only in Buddhism, but in Eastern religions generally, the notion that profound religious experiences consist in a mystical realisation of 'oneness'; a state where we find ourselves completely absorbed in the ultimate reality—Nirvāna, Tao, Brahman and so forth—through the total eradication of our sense of self. In other words, only when we erase all difference between ourselves and true reality can we be said to have succeeded in our spiritual quest. Nothing short of complete unity appears to be acceptable according to this more esoteric way of thinking. The Pure Land school of Buddhism belongs, of course, to the traditions of the East but a general lack of familiarity regarding its teachings has obscured the valuable contribution it has to make to this question of realisation.

Like other depictions of such experience in Eastern religions, Shin Buddhism also speaks of discovering a deep sense of joy and freedom but in the context of an encounter with Amida Buddha. However, an important difference is that we never speak of a vague 'oneness'—the distinction between us and the Buddha always remains firm. From the Buddha's side there may be no difference because, from his enlightened perspective, all reality is indeed a perfect unity but, from where we stand, we can only see ourselves as 'foolish beings of karmic evil caught in birth-and-death, ever sinking and ever wandering in transmigration' as Shan-tao observed. One may ask, 'How can such a person attain enlightenment?; how can such a seemingly negative assessment of human nature be considered the highest form of religious experience'?

The great power of the Pure Land teachings is that they acknowledge and accept ordinary people in all their mental and moral turmoil. They do not insist that we expunge our personal defects before we can be considered fit to follow a spiritual path. In doing so, they represent the pinnacle of compassion in the tradition of Mahāyāna Buddhism. Shan-tao's two-fold definition of 'deep mind' keeps us honest, so to speak. It does this by insisting that we acknowledge—with unflinching candour—that we are foolish beings possessed of muddled minds and that there is little we can do to change that; a recognition that this is what it means to be human and in need of the spiritual emancipation that is offered by the Buddha. At first glance, the message appears to be hopeless, condemning our fractured human nature to endless rounds of rebirth by virtue of our irredeemable karma. And, yet, this is an insight that only makes sense in light of the second part of Shan-tao's definition of 'deep mind'— namely, that Amida Buddha's Vow decidedly grasps sentient beings and that all we need to do is allow ourselves 'to be carried by its power without any doubt or apprehension'.

There are usually two responses to Shan-tao's insight. On the one hand, many will simply not accept such a pessimistic view of human nature—they would vehemently resist the notion that we are bereft of any good that would enable us to attain the highest spiritual goal through our own wisdom. However, what such people forget is that this dire assessment of our nature and abilities—and it certainly is dire—is not possible from mere introspection on our part. Such an insight is only attainable through the illumination of Amida Buddha, which confers the light of wisdom that makes us see what we could not see before. This experience, which we know as *shinjin,* can be shocking and terribly confronting because we are able to see what we really are by viewing our ego-self in the mirror of Amida's true and real mind which he reveals to us.

There is no other way we can come to know this truth about ourselves; we may have intimations of it now and again but the full extent can only be shown to us through the bitter-sweet awareness of shinjin. So, we certainly do not emerge from this experience 'smelling like roses' but we do encounter the truth, a truth that is both painful and liberating at the same time—we cannot secure one without the other as some would like to have it. A saccharine view of human nature can only lead to a sense of betrayal and disappointment, as it is not informed by the highest wisdom which only Amida can bestow.

The other response we find, even among most Buddhists, is: 'What's the catch? How can it be possible to receive this kind of compassionate illumination without having purified ourselves first? Shouldn't we be expending some effort to at least meet the Buddha half-way? Won't we otherwise just become complacent, taking the Buddha's Vow for granted?' These questions betray an inability to fathom the depth of Amida's compassion for suffering beings and his desire to save them. They also demonstrate how little we know about ourselves and the countless trammels that constrain us.

So while it may seem understandable that many might seek to resist the truth of Shan-tao's assessment of religious experience, what we find here is the key to understanding the true meaning behind the notion of 'deep mind'. In other words, we come to see that it is not our mind that is deep or wise but the Mind that is given to us by Amida Buddha; it dwells amidst our own addled consciousness but it does not lead to any kind of vague identity between the two. Returning to the point made at the beginning, religious experience in Shin Buddhism is not about a mystical union where the ego is obliterated, where nothing remains but the Buddha's pure light. On the contrary, we never lose sight of who and what we are—we remain ordinary people but with the difference that we are embraced by Amida without any question as to the extent or severity of our blind passions. Of course, at the time of death, we attain the same enlightenment as Amida Buddha and only then can we be said to have attained a true oneness with this reality.

Until then, however, we are united with the Buddha but without loss of our individuality or karmic separateness. Our fragile humanity remains intact but is immeasurably enhanced through the knowledge of our finitude in conjunction with the insight that we are, despite this, grasped by the power of Amida's Vow—a saving barque that ferries us to the 'Other Shore'. If we allow ourselves to be carried in this way through deep entrusting, we will—as Shan-tao says—attain, without any doubt or apprehension, birth in the Pure Land.

To conclude, it is critical that we understand that our awakening to shinjin, while transformative, is not a self-induced state of constant bliss that eliminates our fallibilities. It does not make us Buddhas here and now. However, it firmly weds us to the Buddha and ensures that we are never separated. In this way, the seed of Buddhahood becomes planted in us, in this life, and will undoubtedly bear fruit when we arrive in the Land of Light. Until then, though, let us take solace in Amida's ever-present and compassionate illumination during our brief but troubled course in this unstable world. This is, indeed, how we are able to perfect the 'deep mind' in the tradition of Shin Buddhism.

Clouds

The light of compassion illumines us always and the darkness of
our ignorance is already broken through. Yet the clouds and
mists of greed, desire, anger and hatred always obscure the sky
of true faith. But though the light of the sun is veiled by clouds
and mists, below them there is still brightness.

The above passage from Shinran has been quoted many times as it
marvellously captures how the power of faith works in the midst of
our blind passions in ordinary life. A few brief reflections will be
offered on this verse to show how it contains the essence of Shinran's
teaching.

From the very beginning, it is made clear that the 'light of compassion illumines us always'. This statement confirms that the light of
Amida Buddha is always constant and unfailing. This is consistent
with the Buddha's 12th Vow that states: 'If, when I attain Buddhahood, my light should be limited ... may I not attain perfect
Enlightenment'. Now, it is because of this that 'the darkness of our
ignorance is already broken through'. In other words, the ever-
present light of Amida is the guarantee that ignorance cannot have
the final word—the power of the Vow breaks the grip of darkness on
our lives. However, this verse makes the even more important point
that this is true even if we do not see it.

The following sentence states: 'Yet the clouds and mists of greed,
desire, anger and hatred always obscure the sky of true faith'. Shinran
observes that our faith is not always pure but that it can, nevertheless,
abide even in the presence of the most ferocious infatuations. Notice
that he uses the word 'obscure' and not a word suggesting that faith is
somehow destroyed or eclipsed by our greed, desire and hatred. This
is a very important insight. Many people worry that unless they
remove these negative characteristics from their hearts, they cannot
possibly make any spiritual progress. Therefore, they cause much
anguish for themselves when they try but fail to do so. Shinran saw the
futility of doing this as well as the needless pain to which it gives rise.

Instead, he encourages us to look at things a little differently. In the
opening lines of the *Kyōgyōshinshō*, he writes:

78

The Universal Vow, difficult to fathom, is indeed a great vessel bearing us across the ocean difficult to cross. The unhindered light is the sun of wisdom dispersing the darkness of our ignorance.

In one of the last works he wrote, *The Virtue of the Name of Amida Tathāgata*, Shinran goes further and says:

Concerning 'unhindered light'—with the light of the sun or moon, when something has come between, the light does not reach us. Amida's light, however, being unobstructed by things, shines on all sentient beings. . . . Amida's light is unhindered by sentient beings' minds of blind passions and karmic evil; hence the expression, 'Buddha of Unhindered Light'. Were it not for the virtue of this unhindered light, how would it be for us?

The notion of Amida's light not being obstructed is critical and helps us to understand the final line from the passage cited at the beginning:

But though the light of the sun is veiled by clouds and mists, below them there is still brightness.

On a cloudy day, we are perfectly capable of seeing things around us quite clearly even though the sun may not be visible. In fact, we know the sun is still there, behind the clouds, otherwise we would not be able to see anything at all but simply be immersed in darkness. The sun allows us to perceive 'brightness' even though it is veiled by 'clouds and mist'. In other words, the sun is 'unhindered' with respect to the various meteorological phenomena that often stand between it and us. It continues to have the power to illumine despite its appearance not being immediately obvious in the sky.

In the same way, the light of Amida Buddha enables us to experience his wisdom and compassion as well as making us see how things are in the world around us and in ourselves. When we feel the full force of our troublesome passions, what makes it possible to see deeply into their reality and effects is, precisely, the Buddha's light that shines on them—otherwise, we would simply endure them without noticing the full extent of their harmful effects. We require a force outside ourselves to help us understand how things really are. This light is Amida's wisdom because it reveals the truth. Without it, we are blind, trapped and helpless.

So even though we often feel discouraged and find ourselves prone to despair in view of the suffering and disappointments we face, as well as the setbacks we often experience in our spiritual lives, it is important to remember that this light remains unhindered throughout all our difficulties. We know this in the same way we know that the sun is still shining even though all we see is 'clouds and mist'. This is possible because we still perceive the 'brightness' around us and so we recognise that its source must be the sun, despite it being obscured from our immediate sight. Similarly, when our lives seem 'overcast' and the presence of the light is not immediately obvious to us, Shinran reminds us that we can know that the sun of Amida's wisdom is always shining, through our awareness of its vivid influence and infallible presence in our hearts.

Religious experience ... is not the acceptance of an opinion, be it ever so true, nor is it believing in dry dogmas or academic abstractions; nor is it to participate in ceremonies. It is a personal experience, it is an insight into the nature of reality, and not a mere emotional thrill or subjective fancy. It is the self integrated into ultimate reality; it has a self-certifying character that carries its own credentials.

Kenshō Yokogawa

PART THREE

Essays

The following essays are revised versions of previously-published articles:

i. 'Jōdo Shinshū: The Supreme Teaching for the Present Age'
[*Shin Buddhist* (No. 11, 2015)]

ii. 'Conceptions of the Absolute in Mahāyāna Buddhism and the Pure Land Way'
[*Light From The East: Modern Western Encounters with Eastern Traditions* (Bloomington: World Wisdom, 2007)]

iii. 'The Dharma of Amida Buddha in the Modern World'
[*The Pure Land: Journal of the International Association of Shin Buddhist Studies* (New Series, No. 20, December 2003)]

iv. 'Reflections on Gensō-Ekō'
[*Mugekō* (No. 1, Spring 1993)]

v. 'Peace as Inner Transformation: A Buddhist Perspective'
[*Religions* (Issue No. 9, 2016)]

Jōdo Shinshū:
The Supreme Teaching for the Present Age

In a world where confusion about values abounds and where many of the old certainties that previously governed our views on life, ethics and religion are crumbling before our eyes, one can be forgiven for feeling lost at sea without any prospect of finding *terra firma*. The spiritual traditions of the world have, each in their own way, endeavoured to provide some kind of anchor to keep us rooted in what is, otherwise, a world of shifting sands. And yet, it seems that many of the traditional faiths find it difficult to keep adherents in the modern world (particularly the West) as the juggernaut of secular humanism encroaches, leaving people bewildered as they struggle to find answers to urgent questions; answers that may appear elusive but which remain critical to our well-being.

There are many theories regarding the crisis of modernity, the collapse of traditional values, the loss of faith and the trivialisation of our public culture. We do not intend to add to those theories here. Instead, it will be suggested how Shin Buddhism is uniquely placed to offer a compelling antidote to the spiritual malaise that afflicts us today and how it is exceptionally suited to give ordinary people the inner resources to confront a world where the 'three poisons' of greed, anger and ignorance are rampant. While certainly not championing the eminence of Shin in any chauvinistic sense, we will nevertheless propose that this tradition is exceptionally capable of meeting our deepest spiritual needs and, in so doing, furnishing our lives with a quiet undercurrent of abiding joy. This can give us the confidence to face the world as it is, even if we cannot change the ineluctable forces that propel our lives in uncertain and troubling directions.

In reflecting on the teachings of the Pure Land master, Hōnen, a contemporary Zen nun once remarked, 'I cannot accept a path that is predicated on the notion of spiritual failure'. I think this goes some way towards explaining a number of the difficulties faced by Shin today: the pervading sense of uncertainty regarding these teachings and the not uncommon feeling of inferiority—that we are somehow not real Buddhists because of our inability to withstand traditional practices. As a result, our commitment to the Dharma has become largely luke-warm and listless. These attitudes have had the debilitating effect of preventing people experiencing the liberation that this Dharma has to offer. The honest recognition of our 'spiritual failure' is, in fact, critical to seeing why this is so.

The aim of this essay is to challenge these misconceptions (and others) with a view to demonstrating how such perceived negatives are actually positives. What makes Shin Buddhism distinctive is its focus on meeting our spiritual yearnings while not neglecting a frank assessment of our human condition—one which entails both obvious, and more subtle, spiritual 'snares'. In terms of day-to-day life, it is precisely these that Shin seeks to bring into sharp relief, as their consequences can be far-reaching. This degree of honesty—very uncomfortable at times—confers true freedom and helps us to avoid the toxic pitfall of spiritual hypocrisy, which is the bane of so much religious thinking today.

Whether we harbour any spiritual beliefs or not, we are searching for truth and certainty; a way of understanding ourselves and the mystery of our existence. This perennial need for answers to such questions cannot be ignored without distorting our humanity in some way and, indeed, doing us an injustice. And, yet, this quest—for those who take it seriously—is fraught with doubt and confusion. People today seem to live in a state of constant apprehension, such that any talk of spiritual matters often seems remote and somehow irrelevant to the struggle of our everyday lives.

Indeed, the modern world seems to reinforce these doubts by denying or denigrating our spiritual needs; by regarding us merely as economic beings whose sole reason for existence is consumption—anything deeper is simply dismissed as fanciful and misguided. Notwithstanding the pervasive influence of these powerful forces that serve to discourage any kind of inner or contemplative life, it is impossible to deny that we are profoundly affected by our impending mortality and the ephemeral nature of things—we desperately seek, in all manner of ways, to find a lasting resolution to this problem.[*]

---

[*] "The crises of modern man are to a large extent religious ones, insofar as they are an awakening of his awareness to an absence of meaning." (Mircea Eliade, 1907–1986)

Why is this so? Why do we often feel there is much more to our existence than what science and secular culture tell us there is? The totalitarianism of the latter in Western society constitutes an aberration—in terms of what people in all cultures have believed for millennia—and, arguably, has led to much unhappiness. So how can we bring all these considerations together to help us gain a better understanding of Shin and its place in the world today? In order to do this, we need to remove some serious misconceptions that plague much current thinking about this tradition.

Firstly, we need to accept—as difficult as this is for some—that Shin (and Pure Land Buddhism as a whole) is a religious phenomenon, not some kind of humanist manifesto which, if true, would render it unintelligible. What gives Shin its undeniable spiritual quality (which it shares with the higher dimensions of the great faiths of humanity) is: (i) its belief in a supreme reality that transcends (but includes) our ordinary world of the senses—a reality that embraces all things and constitutes their essence; and (ii) that awakening to this reality—which has many names (Nirvāna, Suchness, Dharma-Body, Amitābha, Sukhāvati)—is our highest quest as human beings, the purpose of our existence in this life (and any others) as well as the complete fulfillment of our human happiness; none other than the source of our truest felicity.

Now this obvious and, we think, rather innocuous observation is enough to raise the hackles of many who insist that traditional terms which refer to any kind of higher reality, as well as to concepts such as rebirth and karma, are just metaphors employed by less sophisticated people in the past to explain things for which science and modern thought have well and truly found answers.* We are told that Amida is not a real Buddha, that this is just a figurative way of referring to the 'oneness' of humanity and to how we are interconnected with respect to a common (often envisaged as a social) good. Amida's compassion is seen as simply the support we receive from others or

---

* "A religious phenomenon will only be recognised as such if it is grasped at its own level, that is to say, if it is studied as something religious. To try to grasp the essence of such a phenomenon by means of physiology, psychology, economics, linguistics, art or any other study is false; it misses the one unique and irreducible element in it—the element of the sacred." (Mircea Eliade)

the benevolent aspect of the natural world that sustains and nurtures us (conveniently forgetting, of course, its manifold horrors). The Pure Land, it would seem, is nothing more than the state of our minds when purified of their defilements or the ideal form of society where everyone is able to live in peace and harmony.

When viewed in this way, some will insist that Shin is therefore perfectly compatible with a modern and scientific outlook and thus eminently suited to people of today, without any need to believe in outmoded 'myths' and 'fairytales'. Scratch the surface of many a Western Shin Buddhist and this, alas, is what you will find. But, surely, something terribly awry is going on here. This desperate attempt to be seen as 'relevant' and 'contemporary'—whatever that might mean—has led to the wholesale abandonment of the traditional principles on which Shin is founded; leaving us with no more than a tepid and half-hearted outlook that is perfectly compatible with believing in next to nothing—no more, in fact, than the everyday values to which worldly people commonly subscribe.

This mentality is reinforced by a vast array of secondary literature that has rapidly become a substitute for the primary texts themselves. Not that the sūtras and writings of the masters do not require occasional interpretation and commentary but these should be the benchmark by which contemporary works ought to be judged. Interpretation often becomes 're-interpretation' to the point where the power of the original message is lost.

It is also true (and this fuels the problem) that, in this day and age, many people have simply lost their capacity for spiritual insight—the ability to *see* and not just think—into the hidden realities behind this veil of appearances; the kind of direct vision that caused Shinran and his predecessors to sing the praises of the power, light and life that they experienced in their awakening of faith. This is knowledge in the highest degree (and of the deepest truths), not a mere flight of whimsy. Tragically, this capacity has largely been eroded; however— as difficult as this may be—it must be recovered if we are to avoid the spiritual wasteland that awaits us. Take away the eternal verities of this 'power, light and life' that we find embodied in the reality of Amida Buddha, and you are left with nothing.

With the rejection of these truths, we lose the hope that comes with a traditional understanding of the Pure Land. For this life is not all there is. In our most reflective moments (if we are receptive to the Buddha's illumination), we truly sense that this cannot be so and that all of life's loose ends, unfulfilled needs and expectations, as well as its pointless suffering, are inevitably resolved in the realm of enlightenment—Nirvāna, the Pure Land. This is the message that the Buddha taught from the very beginning—namely, that this world is a fleeting, unsatisfying and disturbing miasma that points to something much greater than itself. Otherwise, the Dharma simply makes no sense; what is truly distinctive about it gets lost in the white noise of worldly folly and ambition.* Being kind and thoughtful to others, as well as trying to reduce suffering and injustice, are all very laudable but many non-Buddhists do as much and the Dharma—in all its depth, richness and complexity—is much more than effective social engagement. It is a path of illumination and transformation that aims at the highest of ends—which are not merely ethical or political, but spiritual and thus not entirely of this world.

Now, if we cannot agree on this much, then there is nowhere left to go. If all such talk is dismissed as mere 'fundamentalism' (a label we gladly embrace if taken in its non-pejorative sense of a return to what is *fundamental*) then we are at a dead end. Those who disparage these time-honoured (and tested) traditional understandings might as well throw in the towel—it would be more honest to move on (in light of the implications of what they really believe) and turn their backs on such doctrines altogether, rather than do harm by misappropriating them to exclusively secular ends.

As much as some people are uncomfortable to admit it, they deeply desire salvation. 'From what?' you may ask. From the endless ills, frustrations and cruelties of samsāra along with the myriad poisons to be found in ourselves. If you feel these maladies acutely and cannot seem to find a way through them; if you are prepared to acknowledge the inherent difficulties in eliminating your shortcomings or improving the world around you; if you are serious about

---

* "Life's but a walking shadow, a poor player, that struts and frets his hour upon the stage and then is heard no more. It is a tale told by an idiot, full of sound and fury, signifying nothing." (William Shakespeare, *Macbeth*)

resolving this problem at its root; and if you feel that sense of mystery and beauty in life that beckons you to look beyond what you can see and touch, then the teachings of Shin Buddhism may have something vital to say to you.

It may be useful to turn now to the specific features of Shin that make it such a relevant spiritual path for our times. We will focus on about half a dozen or so themes that exemplify the strengths of this tradition with respect to other options available to people today, thereby demonstrating why this much misunderstood and under-appreciated way offers a universal scope that transcends all cultures, nationalities and human dispositions—no one is excluded from taking this medicine dispensed by the Buddha for our ailing times of crisis and confusion.

(i) *Experiential Confirmation*

As with Buddhism in general, Shin does not demand an uncritical adherence to any doctrinal proposition. Of course, it has doctrines aplenty but these have been developed over the centuries through the collective insights and experiences of its followers, all the way back to Shakyamuni himself; doctrines that have received rich embodiment in the symbolism of the Pure Land tradition.

Shin, in fact, offers itself as an invitation. It says to us: 'Consider the human condition and reflect on the impermanence of all things; listen to the exhortations of the Buddha and taste for yourself the fruits of his compassionate message. If you trust it, then follow in his footsteps'. There is no coercion here; no rejection or condemnation if you spurn the invitation or disagree with what the Buddha is telling you. Just a recognition that one's own karmic maturity may be at a stage where the Dharma vividly speaks to you and can be accepted—and rejoiced in—wholeheartedly.

The Dharma can only emancipate us if we recognise and willingly accept its truth, not because we are threatened with punitive measures. Despite its many hardships and difficulties, human life is considered most precious in Buddhism as it affords the best opportunity (compared to other samsaric states of existence) for realising the Dharma and thus exiting the wearisome round of transmigration once and for all. For this to be possible, we must want to be liberated and accept this as our ultimate good.

Shin encourages us to open our eyes, be guided by those wiser fore-bears who have traversed the path already (as witnessed by the bio-graphical accounts of their powerful and extraordinary experiences) and to accept the compelling evidence of our spiritual intuition as illuminated by the wisdom of the Buddha.

(ii) *Ultimate Reality*

Given that a number of Western Buddhists have come from Chris-tianity (often having fled from unhappy or disappointing experi-ences) it is difficult to broach the topic of a higher or 'divine' reality without provoking a strong reaction—it seems that anything which smacks of 'God-talk' is resentfully dismissed as un-Buddhist. This is rather unfortunate and surely a case of throwing out the baby with the bath-water. Let us be absolutely clear about this: Buddhism does not abandon the notion of an ultimate reality but refines and strips it of many of the troubling limitations that so bedevil certain theistic notions of God. Even from its earliest days, Buddhism recognised a reality that transcended this world—blissful and free from suffer-ing—described (in the early *Samyutta Nikāya*) as:

> ... the far shore, the subtle, the very difficult to see, the unage-ing, the stable, the undisintegrating, the unmanifest, the peace-ful, the deathless, the sublime, the auspicious, the secure, the destruction of craving, the wonderful, the amazing, the unail-ing, the unafflicted, dispassion, purity, freedom, the island, the shelter, the asylum, the refuge....

This is no earthly reality to which one can point. There is nothing in this world of flux, uncertainty and unhappiness that corresponds, even remotely, to such a description. It is quite deliberately depicted as *other*-worldly in that it offers the strongest possible contrast to our world. In this sense, the earlier Theravādin tradition was strictly dualistic—there was Nirvāna (our final goal) and there was this world, with no connection between them whatsoever. When the Mahāyāna began to emerge, its view of Nirvāna became more nuanced and this hard dualism was gradually abandoned. It came to be envisaged under the various aspects through which it was experi-enced: Suchness, Emptiness, Dharma-Body and Buddha-nature. No longer was this reality remote and merely transcendent; rather, it was now seen as dwelling at the heart of all things, such that life and its teeming forms were a reflection of it—its embodiment in the transitory phases of the material universe. Nāgārjuna famously (or perhaps infamously) even went so far as to equate Nirvāna with samsāra in order to make the point that they were inseparable. We are never divorced from this reality as it is all-encompassing while remaining beyond anything we can conceive.

In the Pure Land tradition, the attributes of Nirvāna or the Dharma-Body were developed even further so that they became invested not only with the quality of illuminating wisdom but active compassion as well; a reaching out to suffering beings which are only so many dimensions of itself—hence the indissoluble bond between them. We are able to respond to this compassion in everyday life as a form of awakening (through our saying of the nembutsu) and, at the end of our lives, it becomes the means for returning to our true state. Such a realisation cannot be generated within the confines of our cramped and paltry egos or in the ephemeral concerns of this passing world. This is why it is erroneous to simply identify Nirvāna with the world without any qualification. The world both 'is' and 'is not' Nirvāna ('is not' in the sense of being riddled with ignorance and suffering of which Nirvāna is free and 'is' in the sense that it is a manifestation or 'crystallisation', at a lower level, of this same reality).

In any event, to dismiss certain beliefs because they resemble (in part) something you have already rejected, does not make them false. Yes, Shin does have features in common with other religions (how could it not?) but it also distinguishes itself from them in very important ways that are unique to it. D.T. Suzuki once remarked that all religions have their origin in the Dharma-Body which has dispensed their saving teachings in a way that conforms to the countless needs and limitations of humanity. Indeed, in light of this, some have observed that Shin is, in fact, a kind of summation or essentialised distillation of previous Buddhist teachings.[*]

---

[*] There is an interesting passage that appears in what is, perhaps, an apocryphal account of Shinran when he was a young monk, meeting with a woman who was later to become is wife, Eshinni. Producing from her pocket a crystal burning glass, she said: "Please take this and keep it. It has the power to collect the sun's rays and

Once that which is formless takes on specific forms in which to express itself, it must also assume the deficiencies that come with doing so (and in a plethora of ways according to the endless varieties of human nature) such that differences—often deep-seated—are inevitable. If the highest reality is truly compassionate, it will leave no sector of humankind without guidance and illumination, despite the strife, conflict and mutual incomprehension to which the varied religious forms often give rise. In this sense, much more separates Buddhism from contemporary atheism than it does from other faiths, which—at the very least—acknowledge primacy of the spiritual.

(iii) *Problem of Evil*

A major stumbling block for theistic faith is the difficulty of reconciling the goodness and omnipotence of God with the incomprehensible suffering and unhappiness we find in the world. In fact, one could argue that it is well-nigh impossible. Buddhism offers the distinct advantage of not positing an all-powerful deity that brings creation into being through a conscious act of will. And yet, in the non-dual scheme of the Mahāyāna, the supreme bliss of Nirvāna is not severed from the miseries of samsāra but, clearly, neither are they identical. To be sure, this is a profound mystery at the heart of reality but it cannot be avoided.

A conclusion we can reach is that this world is, in some respects, a manifestation of a better one (that cannot be fully realised in this life and of which the reality of *dukkha* is a constant reminder). Its unsatisfactory nature reflects our 'distance' from Nirvāna while the joy, love and beauty* we do find in this world reveal its luminous presence at the core of everyday life, prompting us to seek a higher awak-

---

focus them on one point, on which it shines with burning heat. Do the same for religion: collect and focus into one point the whole system of the faith, and let that point be made burning and bright, so that it may kindle into zeal even the simplest and most ignorant soul." [Arthur Lloyd, *Shinran and His Work: Studies in Shinshu Theology* (Tokyo: Kyobunkwan, 1910), pp. 64–65]

* "Every beauty that evokes a yearning for transcendence is the fruit of Amida's practice. Beauty is a samsaric expression of transcendent virtue and Amida's stored 'merit' finds its natural expression in beautiful forms" (Chris Morgan, *pers. comm.*). In the preparation of this essay, I am indebted to Mr Morgan for the assistance provided by his many helpful insights.

ening. Evil is a consequence of living in a realm that is evidently not the Pure Land but this world is not, nevertheless, entirely bereft of its light. The existence of suffering is no reason, therefore, to doubt the reality of Nirvāna—our very capacity to see suffering as such, and to want to free ourselves from it, is proof enough of its opposite.*

(iv) *Universal Salvation*

This brings us to one of the most outstanding features of Shin Buddhism: the notion of universal salvation. No other spiritual tradition is as explicit in proclaiming that all sentient beings are embraced spiritually and that all will eventually be released from their current bondage to pain and ignorance.

Amida Buddha is the 'human-facing' dimension of Nirvāna—the accessible aspect of the Dharma-Body that addresses us directly according to our fraught condition. It can do so directly and intimately because, at base, it is our fundamental essence so, by liberating us as individuals, it is also freeing aspects of itself. This is why no one is—or can be—left behind. All that is required is that we accept the working of the Vow which emancipates us, unencumbered by our fretful calculations. And this is where the simple believer, in many ways, has the advantage. A literal belief in Amida Buddha is uncalculating, and allows the nembutsu to penetrate unhindered whereas more sophisticated adherents get bogged down in over-intellectualising faith which leads to a host of fruitless doubts and spiritual paralysis.

Buddhism assuredly has its hells (sixteen of them in fact!) but they are not eternal. Some individual karmas are worse than others and therefore require more radical expiation but, in the end, all beings are destined for the Pure Land. Many will simply refuse to believe this and, indeed, our current age of spiritual myopia strongly encourages us to remain sceptical. Even those who are vaguely attracted to the teachings will say: 'Surely, this is too good to be true'. From the perspective of perfect compassion, however, 'too good' is

---

* "*Dukkha* is a natural consequence of possessing Buddha-nature in the world of birth-and-death. Without *dukkha*, there can be no awakening of faith." (Chris Morgan)

precisely why it is true. Our innate longing to be freed from our mortal fetters is, in fact, the evidence of that which fulfills this very desire. To invoke a cardinal Buddhist law—no effect without a cause.

(v) *Accepting imperfection*

In light of the foregoing considerations, it is easier perhaps to see why the fragile nature of unenlightened beings is no obstacle on the Shin Buddhist path. There is no crippling perfectionism because this is impossible; what is inherently imperfect, can never cease being so. The very conditions that keep us bound in chains of error, greed and anger are essentially ingrained in human nature and in the fact that we inhabit terribly unstable physical bodies riddled with endless desires and infirmities.*

The only response by Amida Buddha to such a state of affairs is profound concern, not condemnation. Therefore, the Buddha has vowed to remove the grievous conditions that bind us—through awakening us to the truth in this life and by guiding us to the Pure Land of Nirvāna when we relinquish our defiled minds and corruptible bodies at the time of death. Hence the emphasis in Shin on lay life; that is, living fully in this world with all our burdens and responsibilities but accepting the reality of our earthly plight honestly, through lives of acceptance, humility and quiet joy without the compulsion to become something we cannot be.

The Buddha does not judge our countless faults, errors, cruelties and insensitivities—creatures of blind passion can do little else.† As an acquaintance remarked to us recently: 'Expecting us not to get wet when we are thrown into the ocean of karma is absurd'.** The only

---

* "Such harmony is in immortal souls, but whilst this muddy vesture of decay doth grossly close it in, we cannot hear it." (William Shakespeare, *The Merchant of Venice*)
† "Never a straight thing was made from the crooked timber of humanity." (Immanuel Kant, 1724–1804)
** "Karma involves countless and imponderable interactions which have ultimately formed our present-day reality in the ocean of birth-and-death. The Dharma is known due to the expedient means of Amida Buddha who is able to render his influence through a perfect reading of samsaric currents. The turbulence of these currents is the very energy used by Amida to draw us near, and then into, the depths where stillness and silence prevail." (Chris Morgan)

response from the 'Other Shore' is compassionate regard and a desire to dispense the necessary cure for our existential sickness. This is what we must consider next.

(vi) *Practice*

In reaching out and making a connection with us, ultimate reality needs to come down, so to speak, from the heights of inconceivable Suchness so that it may be disclosed to us in an intelligible manner.

What better way to announce one's presence than through revealing a name? Amida Buddha, as the compassionate form of formless reality, declares itself to be Unbounded Light and Limitless Life; this we learn through the enlightenment experience of Shakyamuni and the Pure Land tradition which has subsequently confirmed the veracity and efficacy of this most direct of methods.

In the experience of *shinjin,* saying the Name is both the call of Amida Buddha and our response in recognition of this call—in fact, this is really a single event. Nothing else is required. What else, indeed, is possible for ordinary people? When you are lost at sea, and you have the good fortune to encounter a lighthouse, all you can do is follow it as the great beacon guides you to the safety of the shore. What makes this deceptively simple practice so effective is that its consummation is rooted in the Buddha's power which, nevertheless, still requires our acquiescence; we need to admit its light into our hearts if it is to transform us into people of shinjin and, ultimately, into Buddhas.

This great salvific drama is embodied in our hearing, and saying, the Name—*Namo Amida Butsu*. The self-conscious practice of meditation or virtue can add nothing to Amida's working but neither should conventional Buddhist practices be disparaged. Much beneficial activity can emerge, quite naturally, from a life of shinjin but these are its spontaneous expressions, not its conditions. This is practice in its purest form. Initially, it may be difficult, or even painful, given the necessary adjustment required to correct our vanity and self-esteem, but the truth is we cannot genuinely free ourselves; only that which is 'true and real'—from which we are never separated—can do this and bring us back to itself. What is incumbent on us, therefore, is to allow this to happen without our resistance—a faithful yielding to an irresistible force of loving light that will deliver us from this 'burning house' as the Buddha described our world.

(vii) *Wisdom*

While we have given considerable emphasis to the compassionate dimension of the Shin teachings, it is important that we do not lose sight of their 'wisdom' aspect. After all, this tradition's focus on the Buddha's Light is very much about wisdom and its role in endowing us with the illumination of the Dharma. It is what allows us to see things as they really are and as they will always be. In this sense, we must not regard this doctrine as simply confined to the quasi-historical timescale that we find in the sūtras. The Mahāyāna often resorts to symbolic expressions in its sacred literature as if to suggest the numinous, ineffable and timeless aspects of the Dharma.

Many people today struggle to accept the descriptions they encounter in these texts as literally true—something not altogether surprising given the modernist mindset. Nevertheless, we must remain open to the profound truths to which such language points so that it may start working on us.* Imposing manufactured or confected interpretations, based on our flawed calculations, will render the teachings meaningless. This underlines the need to find a good and reliable spiritual friend or guide in the Dharma.

---

* "Symbolism is often misunderstood by modern people. A person of faith may have a completely literal understanding of the Pure Land, Amida and Dharmākara; yet this understanding, at an intuitive and affective level, may have a depth which means that these 'symbols'—though taken literally—are in fact operative within that person. The Mahāyāna is rich in symbolism but one could argue that it is an inspired (in the proper sense of this word) symbolism and, as such, issues forth from the Void itself. We moderns are too sophisticated to take these symbols literally but because we lack the facility, or receptivity, for deep hearing (*monpo*), any penetration into (and the corresponding ability to interpret) these symbols is facile, calculating and misguided. Such interpretations are a hindrance and create a 'block' that prevents Shin's symbols from forming a sacred, and saving, coherence within the practitioner's being. Without this, *monpo* is not possible as Amida's call must compete not only with the background noise of our everyday chaos but also with the mental strain of trying to fit something as vast and deep as the Pure Land tradition, into such a small and shallow mental pigeon hole." (Chris Morgan)

As eternal and infinite, the Buddha's Light is true reality that abides ceaselessly. It works to transform our hearts and minds without thwarting our reason or emotions; rather, it provides an enriching resource for both. The Dharma gives the most penetrating insights that we are capable of grasping with a vision of life that is holistic and connected. It satisfies the intellect and nourishes the spirit, offering genuine fulfillment of our innermost aspirations.

(viii) *Practical value*

There is an increasing tendency to treat the Buddhist teachings as a tool with which to improve our everyday lives. We see a growing focus on its therapeutic value, its ability to help us deal with stress, anxiety and unhappiness, and its potential to address relationship problems or injustices. We see a broken world and we want to 'fix' it. This is most commendable and much good has been done by Buddhists, and others, to alleviate suffering in our society. Clearly, such efforts must always continue unabated. But, of course, one does not have to be a Buddhist to see suffering and feel prompted to address it. Many people in the world are very active and successful in this respect and have no spiritual beliefs or inclinations whatsoever. So, what more does Buddhism offer in light of the pervasive suffering we find in the world?

The Dharma has always taught us to moderate our expectations regarding the world and what it can give. There is no naïve optimism about life and its outlook is thoroughly realistic, always informed by a close observation of the nature of things. Shinran, in particular, was under no illusions about saṃsāra and its limited ability to provide enduring satisfaction, peace of mind or unfettered well-being. In fact, he distinguished these states from a special kind of joy (*kangi*) that derives from spiritual realisation, not something the world can give. This is true bedrock, that which cannot be undermined by the ravages of fortune unlike ordinary happiness. The joy of shinjin enables us to tap into a greater realm from which we can draw sustenance to see us through the unpredictability and disappointments of life.

It is true that there are some Buddhist schools that advocate various practices (for example, mindfulness meditation, tantric rituals and chanting the title of the *Lotus Sūtra*) which aim to harness spiritual energies in order to help improve our human lot. However, there does not appear to be much evidence to support the efficacy of such practices in addressing the unsatisfactory nature of human existence. We will always have sickness, ageing and death to contend with—this is what this *saha* world of endurance is and always has been.

Therefore, attempts to promulgate a view of the Dharma that is entirely this-worldly are bound to fail. We must not be deceived by empty promises and false hopes. Our assessment of the world and human nature should be unflinching. This is more than just being honest—it also implies looking at things with the eyes of wisdom, which are given to us when we awaken to Amida's Light. If we are not interested in the truth, we can choose to ignore it and just busy ourselves with the creation of futile utopias or be distracted by superficial remedies to the real problems that we face.

The truth of the Dharma can seem like bitter medicine at times but it also leads us on a path to spiritual maturity and self-awareness. Wisdom destroys our illusions and purges our ego. There can be no more 'practical' consequences of the teachings—indeed, its fruits are incalculable in guiding our everyday lives.

The great strength of the Shin teaching is that it offers an indirect taste of the Pure Land here and now (in rare moments of grace and lucidity)* while assuring us that our final destiny is the Buddha's realm of utmost bliss. Many will not be satisfied to know that they cannot experience complete emancipation here and now and that they must wait till the end of their lives—but what is this life anyway but a flickering chimera fated to impermanence; an insubstantial blip on the radar screen of the universe; a mere snap of the fingers between two eternities?† And yet, the Buddha's Light shines through it all and shows us where our journey must end.

---

* "Although my defiled life is filled with all kinds of desires and delusions, my mind is playing in the Pure Land." (Shinran, *Jogai Wasan* No. 8)
† "We are such stuff as dreams are made on and our little life is rounded with a sleep." (William Shakespeare, *The Tempest*)

Conclusion & Exhortation

We can see how Shin has inherited the most profound insights of the Mahāyāna tradition, and of early Buddhism as well, while expanding them to encompass the further riches of the Pure Land faith. As mentioned earlier, it is a compelling invitation to abandon oneself* on a journey of spiritual deliverance where true joy can be found.

Therefore, we can only challenge those who hesitate or feel that this path is somehow inadequate or wanting in depth. The only just response in light of this magnificent teaching should be one of gratitude, not insecurity. What other teaching is more suited to the needs of our time and the sober realities of the human condition? Its vision is without peer as is its unconditional acceptance of every sentient being. This blend of breadth, depth and realism is a precious gift and a lasting legacy for the spiritual benefit of generations to come.

For those who believe, with Shinran and his predecessors, that we live in a dark age where confusion and disorder prevail with seemingly no hope on the horizon, the taste of Amida's Dharma is to be savoured like life-giving nectar. We should feel honoured and humbled to count ourselves as wayfarers on this path—privileged, in fact, to have encountered this most rare of teachings bequeathed to us by a succession of compassionate sages who recognised our need for it and who understood, as we must surely realise even more today, that it is the only path left open to us given what we know about ourselves and the world around us. An impartial assessment must reveal that this remains the sole option for nescient beings who find themselves yearning for permanent release from the great round of birth-and-death.

This teaching gives us a gift of wisdom and compassion that transcends impermanence, suffering and doubt. Indeed, there can be no more relevant or universal response to the ills of our time and the ills within ourselves.

---

* It is said that, in the Pure Land tradition, to accept this invitation from Amida Buddha is to fulfill the conditions of the fourth noble truth.

Conceptions of the Absolute in
Mahāyāna Buddhism and the Pure Land Way

A perennial problem for Buddhists has always been the question of how to articulate the relationship between the absolute and relative orders of reality, i.e., between Nirvāna and samsāra. Although conceptions of Nirvāna within the Buddhist tradition have changed over the centuries, it is safe to say that some of its features have remained constant throughout the doctrinal permutations of its different schools. Indeed, some modern scholars of Buddhism in the West have even questioned whether it is meaningful to speak of an Absolute in Buddhism at all, claiming that such a notion is an illegitimate transposition of certain beliefs regarding the highest reality as found in its parent tradition, Hinduism. This essay will attempt to address the question of whether one can legitimately speak of an Absolute in Buddhism, in what such a reality consists and what its implications are for understanding the highest goal of the Buddhist path. In doing so, it will focus chiefly on the Mahāyāna tradition and, in particular, on one of its principal metaphysical texts—*The Awakening of Faith*—in which, arguably, we find one of the most comprehensive and authoritative treatments of ultimate reality in the history of Buddhism.

Early Buddhism was radically dualistic in how it perceived Nirvāna and samsāra—there was simply no connection between them. According to its perspective, an individual could (paradoxically) only attain Nirvāna through the dissolution of this very individuality itself—hence the doctrine of *anattā* or 'no-self'.* Furthermore, there was also the tendency to view Nirvāna more as a state of realisation than any kind of 'being' given the apophatic reticence of early Buddhism to commit itself to any definitive declarations regarding this ineffable reality and, to some extent at least, its conscious desire to

---

* "The Buddhist doctrine of *anattā*—what is its significance but compassion, to lose oneself in others, by realising that a man is not merely a separate individual self but that he is one with others in the Great Reality and that his supreme happiness lies in helping them to attain the Great Realisation of Enlightenment from which flows the Compassion which lightens this and all other worlds." (Beatrice Lane Suzuki, 1878–1939)

demarcate itself from the metaphysics of the *Upanishads*. However, to what extent the polemics between these two camps was simply an outcome of a mutual misunderstanding over the meaning and implications of the concept of *ātman* is a moot point that warrants an entire treatise in itself.

The Mahāyāna perspective

With the arising of the Mahāyāna ('Great Vehicle') as a discrete vehicle of the Dharma in its own right, one witnesses a growing tendency to universalise the concept of Buddhahood as a spiritual principle transcending the human personality of Shakyamuni Buddha, embodying a higher and permanent reality. Hence the concept of the Eternal Buddha which we see promulgated in such central scriptures as the *Lotus Sūtra* and in such fundamental doctrines as that of the *trikāya* or the 'Three Bodies of the Buddha', with the *Dharmakāya* ('Dharma-Body') effectively becoming tantamount to the Buddhist Absolute. Other currents of thought within the Mahāyāna developed this notion further preferring to view the Buddha or Nirvāna as pervading all things, including the totality of samsāra. In time, this growing tendency of attenuating the distinction between the two realms eventually led, especially in the *Madhyāmika* school, to the full-blown identification which we find explicitly formulated in the famous dictum, 'samsāra is Nirvāna'. From the fairly unqualified dualism of early Buddhism we now find a radical non-dualism at the apex of Mahāyāna thinking—and all this under the umbrella of Buddhism. Such a revolution in thinking clearly serves to demonstrate the complexity and controversy inherent in the tradition's struggle to understand the reality of enlightenment.

Having very briefly charted the rudimentary outlines of the transition from the early Buddhist view of Nirvāna, to the more developed and comprehensive conception of the Dharma-Body developed by the Great Vehicle, let us now delve a little deeper into the nature of this Absolute. In one of his earliest works, D.T. Suzuki quotes the following passage from the *Avatamsaka Sūtra*:[*]

---

[*] D.T. Suzuki, *Outlines of Mahāyāna Buddhism* (New York: Schocken, 1963), pp. 223–24.

The Dharma-Body, though manifesting itself in the world, is free from impurities and desires. It unfolds itself here, there and everywhere responding to the call of karma. It is not an individual reality or a false existence but is universal and pure. It comes from nowhere and it goes to nowhere; it does not assert itself nor is it subject to annihilation. It is forever serene and eternal. It is the One devoid of all determinations. This body of Dharma has no boundary and no quarters but is embodied in all bodies. Its freedom or spontaneity is incomprehensible as is its spiritual presence in things corporeal. Assuming any concrete material form as required by the nature and condition of karma, it illuminates all creations. There is no place in the universe where this Body does not prevail. The universe becomes but this Body forever remains. It is free from all opposites and contraries, yet it is working in all things to lead them to Nirvana.

At once, we see a more dynamic and all-encompassing view of ultimate reality possessed of personality, compassion and intelligence which takes the initiative in the liberation of sentient beings. This is in quite stark contrast to the earlier notion of Nirvāna which was more of a static, indifferent and dispassionate reality with no intimate connection to the world of birth-and-death. Nevertheless, both Buddhist traditions would agree that, however conceived, Nirvāna (which is none other than the experiential dimension of the Dharma-Body) remained the ultimate goal of human endeavour and the completion of human fulfillment and happiness. In any case, by personifying the Absolute and in forging a non-monastic path to its attainment, the Mahāyāna opened the gates of the Dharma to all people, especially the laity who had hitherto played a largely peripheral role in the spiritual life.

The Awakening of Faith

In many respects, the culmination of this more positive conception of the Absolute is to be found in a very short, yet profoundly influential, treatise known as the *Awakening of Faith in the Mahāyāna* traditionally attributed to Asvaghosha, although only extant in Chinese. This work, which is often considered as a synthesis of the *Madhyāmika*, *Vijñānavāda* and *Tathāgata-garbha* traditions, has exercised its influence on the founders of all the major schools of the Mahāyāna who have venerated the text as an unimpeachable authority on the questions with which it deals. In that respect, it serves as a very useful and reliable compendium of Mahāyāna metaphysics containing, as it does in a small but terse compass, a range of sophisticated and subtle teaching which one would only come across elsewhere by consulting numerous other sūtras and commentaries where the same points are often made only obliquely.

The fundamental standpoint of the *Awakening of Faith* is its belief in the Absolute which it calls 'Suchness' (*Tathātā*). As we have already seen, this reality has been called by many other names according to the perspective by which it is envisaged; namely, Dharma-Body, Nirvāna, Buddha, Sūnyatā, Bodhi and so forth. Now Suchness, the supreme reality according to this text, is both transcendent and immanent. In other words, it is completely beyond anything that we can imagine or conceive in our world of relativity and yet, at the same time, it comprises the very essence of everything that exists—the 'Ultimate Source'* of samsāra itself. A corollary of this is to say that the Absolute, which is formless, manifests itself through forms which, although finite, are none other than the Absolute of which they are its reflections. This is one way of understanding the meaning of 'samsāra is Nirvāna'. It is not, of course, to say that they are identical but rather that they are ultimately non-dual. In this way, the world around us is then seen as a fusion of the conditioned and the unconditioned. The most illustrious master of the Hua-yen school, Fa-tsang, was a great devotee of the *Awakening of Faith* on which he wrote the most authoritative commentary. His own thought was extensively influenced by this text as is evidenced by the following passage:†

> The very basis of Hua-yen thought seems to be a view of an Absolute which existed prior in time to a concrete world of things which it became. There it was said that any phenomenal object is a mixture of the True and the false, or the Unconditioned and conditioned (of course, the sum total of all things is this same mixture). Taking up the absolute side of things, Fa-tsang says that it itself has two aspects. First, he says, it is immutable. This is not surprising because all religions claim immutability as the nature of the Absolute. What kind of Absolute

---

* *The Awakening of Faith: Attributed to Asvaghosha*, translated, with commentary, by Yoshito S. Hakeda (New York: Columbia University Press, 1967), p. 92.
† Francis H. Cook, *Hua-yen Buddhism: The Jewel Net of Indra* (University Park: Pennsylvania State University Press, 1977), p. 94.

would it be which changed like the ordinary things of the world? Being immutable, the Absolute is forever unmoved, pure, eternal, still and serene. This is, in fact, a common description of the Absolute in all Mahāyāna forms of Buddhism. However, Fa-tsang next says something which not only seems to contradict this statement but which also is very unusual in Buddhism; he says that moved by certain conditions, this pure, unmoved eternal Reality changes and appears as the universe of phenomenal objects. However, like the gold which has become the ring, the immutable Absolute remains immutable. Here the picture is apparently one of the emanation of the concrete universe from an immutable Absolute with the result that things are a mixture of the Absolute and the phenomenal.

This has been quoted at length to show the influence the *Awakening of Faith* had on a major school of Buddhism which, although no longer extant, continues to live through the doctrines and practices of Zen, of which it is the intellectual complement. When the passage mentions this 'very unusual' statement by Fa-tsang, it is referring to none other than the central thesis of the *Awakening of Faith* by which this eminent Hua-yen master was so greatly influenced. The important thing to note, however, is not that this perspective is unusual but rather that it has been rendered so explicitly, since it is a doctrinal position that logically follows from other fundamental tenets of the Mahāyāna.

Another distinctive feature of this text is its stress on the Absolute being both *sūnya* ('empty') and *a-sūnya* ('not empty'). Firstly, "Suchness is empty because, from the very beginning, it has never been related to any defiled states of existence, it is free from all marks of individual distinction of things and it has nothing to do with thoughts conceived by a deluded mind."* Considered in this way, 'emptiness' should not be considered as 'non-existent' but simply (as Yoshito Hakeda, in his commentary, notes) "devoid of a distinct, absolute, independent, permanent, individual entity or being as an irreducible component in a pluralistic world. . . . However, this negation does not exclude the possibility of Suchness being seen from a different viewpoint or order with which one is not accustomed. Hence, there is room to present Suchness, if it is done symbolically, as

* Hakeda, p. 34.

replete with attributes."* Asvaghosha, after declaring that Suchness "was not brought into existence in the beginning nor will it cease to be at the end of time; it is eternal through and through," goes on to say:

> From the beginning, Suchness in its nature is fully provided with all excellent qualities; namely, it is endowed with the light of great wisdom, the qualities of illuminating the entire universe, of true cognition and mind pure in its self-nature; of eternity, bliss, Self and purity; of refreshing coolness, immutability and freedom ... these qualities are not independent from the essence of Suchness and are suprarational attributes of Buddhahood. Since it is endowed completely with all these and is not lacking anything, it is called the *Tathāgata-garbha* (when latent) and also the Dharmakāya of the Tathāgata. . . . Though it has, in reality, all these excellent qualities, it does not have any characteristics of differentiation; it retains its identity and is of one flavour; Suchness is solely one ... it is one without a Second.†

These are critical passages in helping us to understand the nature and function of Suchness. What we see is a concept of the Absolute as, not only the fountainhead of all the happiness, joy and beauty of which we only experience the pale semblances in this life,** but the source of enlightenment and the saving activity of all buddhas and bodhisattvas directed towards suffering beings in samsāra. It is therefore crucial to a proper understanding of Suchness not to view it under its other synonym, namely 'Emptiness' or 'the Void', as meaning mere non-existence—this would be to fall prey to the pitfalls of nihilism which the great Mahāyāna masters always warned us against. Of course, Suchness is not the kind of existence that can be considered analogous to the realities with which we are familiar in our ephemeral world; rather, it possesses a reality far exceeding anything within the purview of our limited empirical existence.

There is a great danger, especially when one reads certain modern studies of Buddhism, in failing to recognise that the notion of emptiness about which one hears so much is not a lack of existence as is sometimes curiously supposed but an emptiness of limitations, rela-

---

* Ibid., p. 36.
† Ibid., p. 65.
** "From one point of view, becoming is a humiliation and, from another, a royal procession." (Ananda Coomaraswamy, 1877–1947)

tivity and delusion. In this respect, emptiness serves as an upāya to help rid us of misguided views concerning the highest reality rather than being some kind of comprehensive statement regarding it. One is inclined to consider the punishing dialectics of Nāgārjuna and his *Madhyāmika* system as simply a form of intellectual therapy designed to remove the obstacles to a clearer understanding of Suchness—breaking through the conventional ways in which we artificially construct what we believe to be reality and to promote a more direct and intuitive mode of awareness through *prajñā* or 'transcendental' wisdom. But such an exercise only stops half-way, otherwise the history of Buddhism would not have witnessed the rise of subsequent schools which endeavoured to fill the gaps, so to speak, left by the purely negative approach of the sūnyatā perspective.

Over time, there developed a growing need for a more affirmative conception of the ultimate reality, one that addressed the fundamental needs of both the intelligence and the will in response to which arose, firstly, the *Vijñānavāda* (also known as Yogācāra) followed by the *Tathāgata-garbha* schools of thought with their emphasis on the positive dimension of the Absolute. Tantric Buddhism can also be considered a response to some of the perceived limitations with the early *Madhyāmika* perspective. In any event, we now find a richer and more complex ontology which sought to integrate existence in its entirety—and at all its levels—with Suchness. No dharma or element of existence was considered to be outside its influence insofar as all reality was suffused with the presence of the Buddha—a notion unthinkable in early Buddhism which was in no real position to reconcile this world of suffering and delusion with the realm which delivered one from all such sorrow. Nevertheless, despite the perplexing nature of the Mahāyāna's preferred way of conceiving the Absolute, it felt that its more difficult perspective was thoroughly justified in view of what it considered to be a deeper awareness of the omnipresent activity of Suchness in our everyday world of samsaric existence.

The Pure Land Tradition

The rise of the Pure Land school was largely contemporaneous with the flowering of the Mahāyāna itself, constituting one of its earliest manifestations. In one sense, it can be argued that the Pure Land way represented the most explicit example of the attempt to render the Buddhist Absolute as accessible as possible to ordinary people through the use of a wealth of rich and positive symbolism designed to heighten the aspiration for enlightenment. In this way, the Pure Land path can also be viewed as the best example of the *a-sūnya* view of absolute reality; that is, in contrast to the Madhyāmikan view of Suchness as 'empty' or the 'Void', it is seen in its fullness and plenitude as the inexhaustible fount of all merits, virtues, wisdom and compassion—an archetypal realm of perfection and beatitude. Hence the traditional descriptions of the Pure Land being replete with the attributes of enlightenment through the evocative symbolism of jewels, music, colours, fragrances and so forth. By employing ostensibly sensual imagery, the sūtras are attempting to convey, in terms that could be readily understood, a sense of the blissfulness of Nirvāna—in contrast, no doubt, to the sense of imperfection that dominates the ordinary world-view of the average devotee. The Pure Land patriarch, T'an-luan, claimed that what distinguished Pure Land Buddhism from other schools is that the 'Dharma-Body of Suchness' (i.e., the formless Absolute) takes the initiative towards suffering beings, manifesting itself as the 'Dharma-Body of Expediency' in the form of various buddhas, bodhisattvas and pure lands but, in particular, the pre-eminent Buddha, *Amitābha* ('Infinite Light').

The Activity of Suchness

Although the Pure Land school claims the dynamic and compassionate nature of Suchness as a major advance in Mahāyāna thinking, it is possible to find the seeds of this conception in the *Awakening of Faith* itself, in its doctrine of 'permeation' (*vāsanā*):[*]

> The essence of Suchness is, from the beginningless beginning, endowed with the perfect state of purity. It is provided with suprarational functions and the nature of manifesting itself. Because of these two reasons, it permeates perpetually into ignorance. Through the force of this permeation, it induces a man to loathe the suffering of samsāra, to seek bliss in Nirvāna and, believing that he has the principle of Suchness within him, to make up his mind to exert himself. . . .

[*] Ibid., pp. 59, 63.

The buddhas and bodhisattvas desire to liberate all men, spontaneously permeating them with their spiritual influences and never forsaking them. Through the power of the wisdom which is one with Suchness, they manifest activities in response to the needs of men as they see and hear them.

This passage clearly shows the omnipresent activity of Suchness functioning as the immanent Absolute working in all things to bring them to enlightenment, to the extent that even an individual's aspiration to seek Buddhahood is brought about by the working of compassionate beings irrespective of whether the aspirant is aware of this influence or not. In this respect, the 'self-power' and 'other-power' debate can be resolved if it is recognised that there is only one power—that of the Absolute—that pervades and supports all things and that one can either accept and remain open to it (by conforming to the Dharma) or allow it to operate unnoticed (by continuing to live in a state of nescience); either way, the working of Suchness, according to the Mahāyāna, will eventually bring all sentient beings to nirvanic fulfillment as there is nothing which does not comprise the Dharma-Body and thereby not immersed in its effulgent reality.

The Significance of Shinran

Finally, we would like to give some brief consideration to the thought of Shinran, and his attempts to reconcile the traditional Pure Land teaching, which he had inherited, with the metaphysical perspective of the Mahāyāna which he would have doubtlessly imbibed as a Tendai monk for twenty years on Mt Hiei. The long-established view of the Pure Land school was that the principal object of devotion was not the formless Dharma-Body itself but the Buddha of Infinite Light (*Amitābha*), formerly a bodhisattva called Dharmākara ('Treasury of Dharma') who, out of compassion for the multitudes of suffering sentient beings, underwent aeons of self-sacrificing practice and austerities which enabled him to accrue sufficient merit to attain Buddhahood and establish a Pure Land, over which he presides, that provides aspirants with an ideal environment in which to pursue the Dharma and attain enlightenment.

For a long time, Amitābha was recognised as one of many buddhas existing throughout the spiritual universe, each with their own Pure

Lands generated from their practices and vows. Devotion to Amitābha, however, was considered particularly efficacious owing to the
fact that his vows were intended specifically for ordinary beings with
little or no spiritual capacity whereas other buddhas had established
certain difficult preconditions for admission to their pure lands.

Shinran, while not explicitly repudiating this traditional view, chose
rather to universalise the symbolism* behind the Dharmākara story
by grounding it in fundamental Mahāyāna principles; partly in order
to address strong criticisms by other sects which considered the Pure
Land way un-buddhistic and partly, no doubt, because he had a profound awareness of a higher reality (which he often refers to as *jinen*
or 'as-it-isness') that he saw as working in all things and manifesting
itself through innumerable compassionate guises such as Amitābha's
Vows and his Pure Land. For Shinran, *jinen* signifies that which is
beyond form and which exceeds the domain of human calculation—
it is the 'Dharma-Body as Suchness' which 'fills the hearts and minds
of the ocean of all beings'.† In one of his famous letters, Shinran
makes the following observation:**

> The Supreme Buddha is formless and, because of being form-
> less, is called *jinen*. When this Buddha is shown as being with
> form, it is not called the supreme Nirvāna (Buddha). In order to
> make us realise that the true Buddha is formless, it is expressly
> called 'Amida Buddha'; so I have been taught. Amida Buddha is
> the medium through which we are made to realise *jinen*.

This passage was written towards the end of Shinran's life and signals
a revolutionary attitude in thinking about the Buddha within the
Pure Land tradition. It is as if Shinran had stripped down the complex and rich edifice of Pure Land spirituality to its foundational
principles. This, however, is not reductionism on Shinran's part but

* "The notion of myth usually evokes a picture of traditional stories charged with a
wealth of symbolism and more or less devoid of historical foundation; however, in
defining myth one should not lay undue stress on this supposed lack of historical
basis for the function of myth is such that, once it has been properly understood,
the question of historicity ceases to have any practical importance." (Frithjof
Schuon, 1907–1998)
† *The Collected Works of Shinran: Volume II* (Kyoto: Jōdo Shinshū Hongwanji-ha,
1997), p. 191.
** *Letters of Shinran: A Translation of Mattōshō*, Shin Buddhism Translation Series,
ed. Yoshifumi Ueda (Kyoto: Hongwanji International Centre, 1978), p. 30.

an attempt to rehabilitate the 'wisdom' aspect of the Mahāyāna that was in danger of possibly being overlooked by the rich upāyas offered by the great message of compassion which, in many ways, formed the centerpiece of the Pure Land message. One also finds in Shinran, and to a greater extent than his own illustrious teacher Hōnen, a more profound appreciation of the multifaceted nature of Nirvāna and its activity:*

> Nirvāna has innumerable names. It is impossible to give them in detail; I will list only a few. Nirvāna is called 'extinction of passions', 'the uncreated', 'peaceful happiness', 'eternal bliss', 'true reality', 'Dharma-Body', 'Dharma-nature', 'Suchness', 'Oneness' and 'Buddha-nature'. Buddha-nature is none other than Tathāgata. This Tathāgata pervades the countless worlds; it fills the hearts and minds of the ocean of all beings. Thus, plants, trees and land all attain Buddhahood. Since it is with these hearts and minds of all sentient beings that they entrust themselves to the Vow of the Dharma-Body as 'Compassionate Means', this shinjin is none other than Buddha-nature.

Shinran here is advocating a broader grasp of Nirvāna than we see in any of his Pure Land predecessors even though he was greatly influenced by them in arriving at his developed position. Amitābha, therefore, becomes the compassionate personification of Suchness itself and not simply the outcome of the innumerable practices of a particular quasi-historical individual over many aeons. Even Dharmākara himself, according to Shinran, emerges from the ocean of Suchness to make known the vows of the Buddha of Infinite Light through the sūtras of the Pure Land tradition. Furthermore, he takes the radical step of equating the true Pure Land with Nirvāna itself rather than treating it as a more favourable abode for Buddhist practice, so that to attain birth in the Pure Land is, essentially, attaining enlightenment. Similarly, in relation to the central experience of the religious life according to Shinran, i.e. shinjin, we no longer find just a rudimentary faith in the Buddha and his power to save but a recognition that this experience has its source in the very heart of reality itself—another way of saying that awareness of the Buddha's working through the experience of shinjin is none other than the activity of the Buddha himself in sentient beings.

* *The Collected Works of Shinran: Volume I* (Kyoto: Jōdo Shinshō Hongwanji-ha, 1997), p. 461.

The Unhindered Path

Shinran was acutely conscious not to be seen as indulging in unorthodox innovations which is why he went to such pains to cite authoritative scriptures in support of his views. On the one hand, he needed to convince other Mahāyāna sects that his teaching was not a distortion of the Dharma and, on the other, he had to assure those within the Pure Land school that he was not being unfaithful to its perspective either. The extent to which he succeeded in accomplishing this challenging task is evidenced by the extraordinary flourishing of the Jōdo Shinshū over the past seven hundred years. One of the principal texts that Shinran used in support of his views regarding the highest reality was the famous *Nirvāna Sūtra* which he quotes extensively in his *magnum opus*, the *Kyōgyōshinshō*. In order to reinforce the point about the unanimity between Shinran and the great metaphysical insights of the Māhayāna tradition, which he deeply venerated, some brief but important passages from the *Nirvāna Sūtra* follow below.* Shinran cites these with approval and they serve to demonstrate, not only that he is thoroughly faithful to this tradition in his view of ultimate reality, but that he accomplished a remarkable synthesis between the respective demands of wisdom and compassion in his propagation of the Pure Land faith:

> Tathāgata is also thus: non-arising, non-perishing, unageing, undying, indestructible and incorruptible; it is not a created existence.... All created things are impermanent.... Buddha-nature is the uncreated; hence it is eternal.

> The Tathāgatas are eternal and never changing; hence they are termed true reality.

> Although sentient beings are impermanent, still their Buddha-nature is eternal and unchanging.

> The Dharma-Body (of the Tathāgata) is eternity, bliss, self and purity.

Conclusion

In closing, we would like to reiterate the great importance of an adequate and satisfying conception of the Absolute as being indispensable to the Buddhist path. In a climate of increasing scepticism and reductionism, especially in many scholarly circles, it is imperative

---

* *Collected Works: Volume I*, pp. 181, 184–85, 188.

that we not lose sight of the fact that without such concepts as the Dharma-Body, Suchness, Nirvāna and Sūnyatā being grounded in a true reality that both transcends and suffuses all things, Buddhism is left without any foundations and stands on nothing, thereby losing all soteriological efficacy. In the attempt by some to make Buddhism more fashionable by denying that it has anything much in common with views of ultimate reality in other spiritual traditions, it does itself a great disservice in failing to recognise clear parallels where they exist—parallels, indeed, that should not surprise anyone. To dismiss all these terms used to depict the Absolute as merely 'symbolic', as if to downgrade their significance, is folly—of what exactly are they symbols? To be sure, these terms do not exhaust the fathomless depth of the reality to which they refer but, on the other hand, neither are they ciphers created by us in order to fulfill a nostalgic but delusory quest for the Infinite, without having any basis in the true nature of things. A spiritual path that cannot secure deliverance from what is finite, imperfect and illusory, thus ensuring eternal blessedness and the end of suffering, is simply not worthy of the name.

The Dharma of
Amida Buddha in the Modern World

Because the power of the Vow is without limits,
Even our evil karma, so deep and heavy is not burdensome;
Because the Buddha's wisdom is without bounds,
Even the bewildered and wayward are not abandoned.

(Shōzōmatsu Wasan)

It should be readily apparent, to those familiar with the perspective of Shinran, that it is, first and foremost, a teaching for the 'bewildered and wayward'; the spiritual emancipation of which is the primary focus of the Pure Land tradition. It is also important to acknowledge that Shinran was not interested in social reform *per se*, and that any political application of his teaching is secondary, if not altogether irrelevant, to his primary purpose:

> Concerning compassion, there is a difference between the Path of Sages and the Pure Land Path. Compassion in the Path of Sages is to pity, commiserate with and care for beings. It is extremely difficult, however, to accomplish the saving of others just as one wishes. Compassion in the Pure Land Path should be understood as first attaining Buddhahood quickly through saying the nembutsu and, with the mind of great love and compassion, freely benefiting sentient beings as one wishes. However much love and pity we may feel in our present lives, it is hard to save others as we wish; hence, such compassion remains unfulfilled. Only the saying of the nembutsu, then, is the mind of great compassion that is thoroughgoing. (*Tannishō*)

Our current age, like any other, faces its own unique problems and challenges. However, the perennial concerns of salvation and enlightenment have remained constant throughout the ages. Buddhism, along with other faiths, appears to be going through a crisis of identity in the modern era. In fact, there is an increasing tendency today to call to account all spiritual traditions with respect to their social relevance. In other words, traditions are judged as 'useful' to the extent that they are capable of guiding people in their social and ethical conduct. Any religious path that seems too 'other-worldly' is dismissed as of little value in the face of the imperious demands of modernity. This same tendency is now gaining a foothold in Jōdo Shinshū.

Essays

The phenomenon of 'socially-engaged' Buddhism is currently seen as the new direction that must be taken if the Dharma is to maintain any pertinence for people today. It is commonplace these days to play down the other-worldly tenor of the Pure Land tradition as it if were largely irrelevant, but to do so would be to grossly distort its teachings. Traditional ideas regarding the spiritual life, transcendent reality or the posthumous states of existence are being abandoned as regressive and outmoded, seeing that some modern exponents of Buddhism prefer a more this-worldly *raison d'être* for the teachings of Shakyamuni. What are the implications of this quantum shift in apprehending the Buddhist path?

There is much talk about the need to manifest compassion in the world as the most effective way of practicing or demonstrating our faith. However, we need to be clear that such manifestations can be both very limited and misguided. In Shin Buddhism, we also have to be careful not to advocate the practice of compassion with a view to a selective socio-political agenda or, more critically, with the aim of setting some kind of benchmark for determining authentic *shinjin*. In other words, there is a danger in suggesting that the mind of faith should manifest itself in certain types of behaviour or ethical conduct, or that it ought to be qualified on the basis of social considerations. We often hear that the essence of the Dharma is 'kindness'. Well and good, but is the person of shinjin always kind? Is it inconceivable that such an individual cannot be, for example, racist or homophobic? Assuredly, most of us would strongly disapprove of such prejudices but can we say that people who harbour them are not individuals of true faith? If not, how do we understand Shinran's references to our being 'burdened with deep and heavy evil karma'? To what can this refer except to thoughts and views that are harmful to both ourselves and others? On the other hand, should we always assume that people who appear to be kind and compassionate necessarily manifest Amida's working?:

> We should not express outwardly signs of wisdom, goodness or diligence for, inwardly, we are possessed of falsity. We are filled with all manner of greed, anger, perversity, deceit, wickedness and cunning, and it is difficult to put an end to our evil nature. In this, we are like poisonous snakes or scorpions. (*Kyōgyōshin-shō*)

In any case, it is far from obvious that kindness is, in fact, the essence of the Dharma or that it can be treated as, in any way, synonymous with compassion which is an altogether different order of virtue.*

The question comes down to this: Do we need a spiritual underpinning to our moral actions? Many individuals, who adhere to no religious beliefs whatsoever, are perfectly capable of behaviour that is considered beyond reproach, whether it be valorous, compassionate or self-sacrificing. Confucianism, Aristotelianism and, more recently, Consequentialism, are just some examples of highly-regarded ethical systems that do not have any religious basis. A further question thus presents itself: Does having shinjin lead to more compassionate behaviour? The answer must surely be 'Not necessarily'. It may certainly make one more deeply and painfully conscious of one's lack of true compassion but this does not, as a matter of course, entail becoming a 'better' person in the conventional sense—in other words, it does not dispel one's 'bewildered and wayward' nature.

It is also true that people who have been awakened to the reality of Amida Buddha through shinjin can sometimes spontaneously manifest extraordinarily benevolent behaviour but this is never affected, contrived or calculated. It has no objective in mind but is simply a by-product of the profound joy that is felt in this awakening. Nevertheless, such behaviour should not always be taken as a sign of shinjin. The only compassion that is pure and unadulterated is that which flows from Amida Buddha himself and which is able to encompass all beings despite their weaknesses.† The true end of the spiritual life is not simply to make our worldly life more just or harmonious—one can do as much without any reference to religion. To

---

* "In the sense intended by the Dharma, compassion is no mere kindness (that is to say, fellow-feeling) but . . . can only occur on the part of those who have understood and transcended the illusion of self, whereby there is a kind of identification with the other. It just never seems to have occurred to Shinran that such a state of mind could be contrived by an ordinary person like himself." George Gatenby— 'True Compassion', a commentary on *Kōsō Wasan* No. 35 (www.georgegaten by.id.au/kw35.htm). The author would like to extend his gratitude to Reverend Gatenby for his invaluable advice in the preparation of this essay.

† "Compassion must be aligned with wisdom, lest it be misguided. Sometimes a kind of violence is required in the name of greater compassion. For example, the intrusive and painful treatment for cancer may seem cruel if we do not understand

insist that religious ideas can only be useful if they serve social ends serves to disfigure the goal that such notions have in the first place; namely, to awaken people to a realm that transcends the suffering and anxiety of this world (which is just as often caused by the very moral and social attitudes that many seek to impose on others of a different persuasion). There is nothing absolute or enduring about worldly values. This is not to say that they cannot assist in social cohesion when implemented wisely (all too rarely alas) but they are, nevertheless, too unstable to serve as a benchmark by which to judge the efficacy of the Buddha's teaching.

One sometimes gets the impression that the 'engaged Buddhism' agenda is distinctly calculated to cultivate particular moral or social outcomes without questioning whether these are always helpful or desirable. Ethics is a deeply ambiguous realm of human endeavour and one should be wary of speaking in absolutes here, especially when the facts are unclear. Of course, in a very obvious sense, the world is desperately in need of greater levels of sympathy and under-standing but such qualities can only arise naturally and not as part of a program dedicated to Buddhist activism. Otherwise, they will be seen to be hollow virtues backed by nothing more than an artificial 'moral planning' that seeks to contrive what it thinks best in each sit-uation, usually on the basis of a predetermined ideology.

What gives us the confidence to make bold assertions about the well-being of society and its members? Any pronouncements of this kind should be tempered by a profound humility and a sense of our own shortcomings. What is being questioned here is the necessary link between faith and a certain kind of moral outlook. To insist on such a nexus is to deprive shinjin of its universality and efficacy. We should not be intimidated by the demands of other spiritual tradi-tions which insist that religious faith must assume particular moral paradigms in order for such faith to be validated:

the reason for it. Or protecting the vulnerable may require force that, at face value, may seem opposed to compassion. Bodhisattvas can often take wrathful forms in protecting the Dharma, or as a manifestation of compassionate means. We lack the wisdom to be able to effectively understand what true compassion is and, because of this, what we believe to be compassionate action can often result in greater harm." (Chris Morgan *pers. comm.*)

> Being without even the slightest love or compassion, how could
> I hope to benefit sentient beings? (*Shōzōmatsu Wasan*)

The Buddha undoubtedly prescribed many ethical and meditational
precepts. These included kindness, compassion, tolerance, love, gen-
tleness as well as wisdom, concentration and fortitude. In doing so,
he hoped to have us dispel the 'three poisons' of anger, greed and
ignorance which only serve to compound the vices of our ego and
our ability to see things as they really are. However, the Buddha's prescriptions were not merely ends in themselves. They served a higher
purpose which was to rescue people from the self-inflicted maladies
that leave them frustrated, disappointed, directionless and in despair.
No amount of 'good-will' can address these challenges unless it can
also serve to lead us to an awareness of ultimate reality. All seemingly
altruistic or generous activities are limited; either by our own failings
or by restrictions in circumstances. Often they are also tainted by our
selfish desires, however subtle these may be:

> People of this world are preoccupied with thoughts that are not
> real.... Even those who renounce this world think of nothing
> but fame and profit. Hence, know that we are not good persons,
> nor persons of wisdom; that we have no diligence, but only
> indolence, and that within, the heart is ever empty, deceptive,
> vainglorious and flattering. We do not have a heart that is true
> and real. (*Yuishinshō-mon'i*)

All attempts at improving our lot in this world, while highly laudable, are inadequate to address the root causes of our existential crisis. Needless to say, no one is suggesting that people ought not to be
more thoughtful and caring towards others—on the contrary, we see
nowhere near enough of these virtues in the world. The point is that
the ultimate aim of any spiritual path has little to do with any kind of
moral or social activism. In as much as the world is often afflicted
with profound self-deception, we need to be aware—as Shakyamuni
pointed out—that sentient beings and their activities are similarly
impaired. Social values are fluid, changeable and often contradictory.
There is nothing inherently dependable in society's mores or ethical
norms. While they serve to make life tolerable and serve a utilitarian
purpose, they are no substitute for the profound spiritual relief we
attain from a direct experience of the eternal reality that we come to
know as Amida Buddha.

As indicated above, the Dharma certainly provides ethical prescriptions such as the precepts, the eight-fold noble path and the six pāramitās. When practised in a completely disinterested manner, such virtuous actions can certainly prove morally and spiritually efficacious—but how many of us are actually capable of acting in this way? In almost all cases, our behaviour, however much it may appear driven by moral objectives, is often motivated by subtle forms of self-interest. Genuinely compassionate behaviour is the exception and no doubt rarer than we imagine. It may well be that Amida's light occasionally breaks into our hardened egos and then shines through into the world as a genuine instance of unaffected tenderness or kindness; this, of course, cannot be denied. However, to what extent can this be the subject of exhortation or the foundation of a program for social reform?

One often hears that the Dharma provides us with a deeper insight into the nature of such qualities as compassion through our personal experience of Amida's embrace and through the teaching of interdependence. It is indeed true that the life of shinjin does open up illuminating spiritual vistas for the individual. Nevertheless, it does not follow that the realisation of, say, shinjin or pratītya-samutpāda must lead to some kind of corresponding urge to address the ills of the world. It certainly can but the fact that it may not should not count against the veracity of such a realisation. As ought to be clear by now, we are not trying to condone any kind of moral indifference towards the many, tragic problems that plague human societies. Neither are we excusing morally reprehensible behaviour. One needs to remember Shinran's distinction between acts that are a consequence of 'blind passion' and those that are deliberately calculated to hurt others. It may well be that genuine instances of wilful and premeditated malice or cruelty are inconsistent with a mind of shinjin, but this is not the point.

An 'engaged' form of Buddhism, while well-intentioned, harbours the very real possibility of causing a certain measure of spiritual harm to those who find themselves unable to conform to the 'engaged' agenda; which is precisely what it is. An agenda that has nothing immutable about it and which only reflects the passing preoccupations, viewpoints and biases of its age. Indeed, one wonders how relevant (or even recognisable) the current form of engaged

Buddhism will be in one or two hundred years' time. If anything, such a contrast may very well serve to demonstrate the fleeting nature of our current concerns. One really has to ask whether Shinran had any sense of social engagement of the kind envisaged by its modern exponents. What Shinran *is* engaged with is Amida Buddha and his Dharma, not with transient values which have no bearing on his final goal of emancipation. Without doubt, he was acutely aware of the many injustices around him as well as the deep-seated moral and spiritual hypocrisy of his contemporaries but he never sought to have his faith act as a kind of catalyst for social transformation. On the contrary, he pointed to the many evils of his time in order to encourage people to turn their minds from worldly matters and focus on the nembutsu path. One fears that in our rush to seem 'relevant', we are putting the cart before the horse. Are we so confident that we have adequately addressed all the spiritual questions and problems that are posed by Shinran, that we can now safely move on from such concerns and busy ourselves with issues of 'application', however that is conceived? Many people today are still clamouring for bread and are only being given stones. This fact may, perhaps, go some way towards explaining the decline in religious faith, not only in Shin Buddhism, but in other spiritual traditions as well.

The life of shinjin is, without question, a spiritual path aimed at the attainment of enlightenment and the liberation from samsaric bondage. Its social import is really neither here nor there. If the Dharma cannot illuminate and nourish you spiritually in its own right, then no degree of 'engagement' is going to suffice or take its place. One is tempted to think that the excessive emphasis placed on engaged Buddhism masks a kind of agnosticism or, at worse, a spiritual bankruptcy with respect to matters of faith. It is as if, in this 'Decadent Age of the Dharma', the purely spiritual and contemplative aspects of the path have been abandoned and replaced by a restless activism that seeks to transform the world into something it can never be. Intra-samsaric solutions are not the answer. Unless you solve for yourself the fundamental question of 'birth-and-death' (a lifetime's work to be sure), you will never be capable of any genuinely beneficial action in the world. The most important such action or outcome is attaining shinjin for oneself and sharing it with others. This is difficult enough without also attempting to establish a further requirement to make this activity 'relevant to our times' or making it a foundation for social improvement—a precarious exercise to say the least.

The other point that needs to be made is that people of shinjin are perfectly capable of having profoundly opposed positions in relation to moral, social and political questions. The *Myōkōninden*, for example, tells of devout Shin followers who manifested a variety of dispositions with regard to society, although mainly quietist and conservative.

> We who aspire for Amida's fulfilled land,
> Though we differ in outward condition and conduct,
> Should truly receive the Name of the Primal Vow
> And never forget it, whether waking or sleeping.
> (*Kōsō Wasan*, verse 96)

There is a need for a ruthless honesty and critical self-examination with regard to any kind of imposition of values that are somehow seen to be self-evident. This is often far from being the case and pernicious results may ensue if we are oblivious to this fact. Are we then to have no benchmark for guiding our behaviour in the world? The doctrine of *ahimsa* ('non-harming') has always been a compelling notion that has guided Buddhists since the dawn of this tradition. The belief that we should not cause harm to sentient beings can usually be discerned at the heart of many moral doctrines as it draws on the Buddhist teachings of compassion and the inter-dependence of all beings. The concept of *ahimsa* can inform a number of our activities in the world (e.g. law and order, welfare policy, sexuality and so on) but even then, the fair and accurate application of this principle is rarely straightforward and can often be mired in deep uncertainty (such as balancing competing forms of harm and establishing degrees of acceptable suffering, for example).

Buddhist models for behaviour are profoundly instructive and are clearly inspired by the Buddha's insight into our tragic human condition, as well as by his compassionate concern to alleviate our suffering. Such models can serve as helpful guides, however short we may fall with respect to these standards. They provide critical touchstones for showing us whether we are heading in the right direction but it is not always clear that they will provide a satisfactory solution in every case. The realm of human values is marked by obscure and hard-to-fathom motives as well as considerable self-interest, despite the possibility of occasionally being able to see our way through to a more objective and disinterested position. Even so, we must be careful not to use spiritual insights (which are not always amenable to adequate verbal formulation) as a catalyst for initiating social or political commentary where this is only likely to fuel confusion, uncertainty and resentment.

The world is full of opinions on questions of moral importance and it is well-nigh impossible to establish any kind of unanimity or consensus on such matters even among people who share the same spiritual beliefs. Accordingly, it is hardly desirable to insist on uniform demands for our engagement with the world. The realm of saṃsāra can never provide us with these kinds of certainties and we would do well to honestly admit this rather than think we were doing something useful in prescribing criteria for rectitude in matters of faith based on whether such faith has been appropriately applied and translated into some form of engagement with our society.

Despite Shinran's negative assessment of human nature, it is somehow comforting in that it boldly affirms certain realities that cannot be overlooked, including the fact that we are all, in one way or another, afflicted by countless obstacles in the quest for human fulfillment. His assessment forces us to pause and reflect on the nature of the world, its often specious values, artificial expectations and spurious demands. It also helps us to see the appalling suffering, injustice and tragedy in the world (much of it unnoticed by most of us) as well as the ignorance, cruelty and futility of so many ventures that seek to improve perceived wrongs and injustices.* Shinran also helps us to acknowledge the confronting truth that we invariably contribute to this sad state of affairs despite our best intentions. To gloss over these facts is to fail to understand what it means to endure life in this world of transience, pain and disappointment.

Our lives can be cut short in the blink of an eye. Our influence is limited and we are flawed as moral agents. This was the Buddha's realistic appraisal of the situation in which we find ourselves, and it would be unremittingly pessimistic if he did not also show us a way out of

---

* "When we are born, we cry that we are come to this great stage of fools." (William Shakespeare, *King Lear*)

this existential impasse; not through engaging with the world but by transcending both it and ourselves. This is our primary objective in following the Pure Land path—the attainment of Nirvāna and the liberation of all sentient beings from the brutal ordeal of birth-and-death (at least to those for whom such concepts are still meaningful). The person who has been blessed with the realisation of shinjin may act as they see fit confident in the knowledge that their salvation is assured. They may thus manifest kindness, anger, mercy or lust as conditions and individual karma dictate but always with the full awareness that they are 'bewildered and wayward' yet fully embraced by Amida Buddha. This is the goal of Shin Buddhism in this life to which all our endeavours should be directed. Nothing else can be as important because without it, all our other efforts and aspirations are in vain. This may sound unduly passive but, in essence, our most important task in this life is the awakening to Amida's Mind in the realisation of shinjin. The experience of many Pure Land adherents over the ages has been one of finding ourselves in this inhospitable world as if banished from our true home to which we yearn to return. This calls for a certain measure of extrication from the world, not a total engagement with it at the expense of our spiritual priorities. In the memorable words of Shan-tao:

> Let us return! Do not abide
> In this homeland of māras.
> Since innumerable aeons ago
> We have been transmigrating,
> And nowhere has there been any pleasure;
> We hear only the voices of grief and sorrow.
> After this present lifetime has ended,
> Let us enter the city of Nirvāna! (*Kyōgyōshinshō*)

We must be allowed to be guided by our own lights and conscience in our relations with the world and also to make mistakes in doing so. Neither should we always be judged for failing to act in ways expected of us by others or for refusing to conform to particular ethical or social assumptions that are, in any event, likely to be far from self-evident. In such instances, we would do well to avoid the traps of self-righteousness and hypocrisy.

We also need to honestly acknowledge the morally agnostic tenor of Shinran's outlook:

> But for a foolish being full of blind passions, in this fleeting world—this burning house—all matters without exception are lies and gibberish, totally without truth and sincerity. The nembutsu alone is true and real. (*Tannishō*)

Any attempt to overlook this truth or to somehow sanitise it is, arguably, a betrayal of his teaching.

This essay has not aimed to present a purely academic exposition of its theme. In view of the exigencies of the matter, it is more of an exhortation to focus on priorities. In Shin Buddhism today, there appears to be scant regard to the *inner* engagement that we each must have with Amida Buddha. Our actions in the world will be an outcome of this encounter and of our personal karma, and no one is in a position to predict it, let alone prescribe for it. The endless variety of human temperaments and dispositions must be respected and accommodated in any world-view that individuals may form, even if we disagree or have little sympathy for it.

Shin Buddhism is a spiritual tradition and a profound one at that. It does not constitute or imply a specific social ideology and does not envisage an ideal state of affairs for the world over and above its spiritual aims. Shinran certainly expressed sincere hope for the spread of peace in the world—who would disagree with him?—but this is just an aspiration and not a formula for success. In the modern age, one often hears the complaint that religion has to adapt to the 'ways of the world'. The modern world, with its chaotic confusion of prejudices and misguided aspirations, represents nothing of absolute value when considered *sub specie aeternitatis* ('under the aspect of eternity'). It is not for the Dharma to conform to the world but for the world to conform to the Dharma.

Reflections on Gensō-Ekō

A paramount theme in the thought of Shinran is his profound concern that our individual salvation not be considered apart from the aspiration to save all beings. In keeping with Amida's Primal Vow, where the Buddha declares that he will not enter Nirvāna unless he can emancipate all suffering creatures, Shinran exhorts a comparable attitude in the follower of the Pure Land way. Any personal liberation divorced from that of others is considered contrary to the spirit of great compassion which Amida himself extends to us all. Accordingly, Shinran does not view Nirvāna as a blissfully self-absorbed state of repose where one remains oblivious to the harrowing plight of those left behind:

> When a person becomes enlightened, we say they 'return to the city of Dharma-nature'. It is also called realising true reality or Suchness, realising the uncreated or Dharma-Body, attaining emancipation, realising eternal bliss...and attaining the supreme enlightenment. When persons attain this enlightenment, with great love and great compassion immediately reaching their fullness in them, they return to the ocean of birth-and-death to save all sentient beings. (*Yuishinshō-mon'i*)

In stressing this attitude, Shinran is rehabilitating a theme first advocated by Vasubandhu and, after him, Tan-luan, but largely overlooked by subsequent Pure Land masters. Shinran was concerned to bring out the ramifications of the bodhisattvic idea that one's desire for enlightenment is the aspiration to save all beings. *Gensō-ekō* then, is the 'phase-of returning to this world of evil passions' in order to save others after one has, oneself, been born in the Pure Land and attained Buddhahood.

A quandary, however, immediately presents itself: if Amida is all sufficient for our salvation, what need of bodhisattvas and other buddhas to accomplish the same end? To suggest that we need to return to this world to save others implies that the salvific power of Amida is somehow wanting or deficient; surely an untenable proposition. Amida, 'Buddha of Immeasurable Light', does all the work for our attainment of enlightenment; which is why, precisely, he is the sole object of reverence in the Pure Land tradition. Veneration and worship of other buddhas is firmly eschewed in this tradition and for good reason; Amida alone has unconditionally vowed to save all karma-burdened creatures and no other support for enlightenment is required. Amida, as the supreme and merciful manifestation of the uncreated Dharma-Body, is the only true and absolute reality there is, and surely no other recourse than the very highest is necessary for our deliverance.

The other point to consider is this: Shinran often suggests that when we enter the Pure Land at death, we pass directly into Amida's reality. In other words, in attaining the same Buddhahood as Amida, we, in a certain manner of speaking, *become* Amida Buddha. Nirvāna is, pre-eminently, the realm of non-duality where separateness of any kind no longer prevails. Absolute reality is the unified realm of the Dharma-Body or Suchness itself; it harbours none of the unstable flux that is part and parcel of this samsaric world. If we can accept this, then it becomes difficult to envisage, literally, the traditional notion of the Pure Land as a place populated by individually distinct bodhisattvas who are constantly returning to the world of 'birth-and death' in order to rescue the ignorant and the suffering. Absolute reality is a dynamic entity. It emerges from its own formless essence ('Dharma-Body as Suchness') so that it can assume 'name and form' ('Dharma-Body as Compassion') for the sake of afflicted beings. This, of course, is who we know as Amida.

How then, do we reconcile the traditional point of view regarding *gensō-ekō* with these considerations? To say that 'we'—as individuals—return should not be taken at face value; after we attain union with the Dharma-Body at death, we return *as* Amida; or rather, in our 'capacity' as Amida. After all, Shinran often reminds us that Amida constitutes our true self; our latent Buddha-nature which is only fully realised in the Pure Land and is the real source of all 'personality'. During our sojourn through life, this wonderful treasure we harbour deep within us remains largely veiled, not only by our *skandhas* which determine our individual constitution, particularity and karma, but also by the myriad blind passions that obscure our Buddha-nature and keep us firmly bound to the wheel of samsāra. At death, the person of shinjin, through the inconceivable working of Amida, is caused to sever all the bonds that separate them from their true essence; which is none other than absolute reality itself—Nirvāna. In the *Jōdō Wasan*, we read:

Buddha-nature is *Tathāgata* ... *Tathāgata* is *Nirvāna* ... *Nirvāna* is called Buddha-nature.

On entering the Pure Land we can say that we 'are like river waters that, on entering the ocean, become one in taste with it' (*Songō Shinzō Meimon*). There can no longer be any room for separate personalities in such a realm. Non-duality can only properly admit of one reality: namely Amida with whom, in our core identity, we are undivided, despite the existential taints of our forlorn condition in this life. If not for this essential affinity, there would be no means of communion between ourselves and the Buddha.

None of the foregoing observations should come as any real surprise. They are entirely consistent with the Mahāyāna perspective of non-duality, and to take it seriously one is logically compelled to draw the above conclusions concerning our status in the after-life. If the highest spiritual state that is possible for us is union with ultimate reality or the Dharma-Body, in the form of Amida, then there can be little room for anything else; all other ostensible realities (by comparison) being false and illusory products of samsāra. Similarly, then, it must completely suffice as both our sole object of faith and complete cause of enlightenment.

Why, then, do we get this strong insistence in the scriptures on *gensō-ekō* as traditionally understood? I think we may be able to understand it in the following way. The impetus underlying the doctrine of *gensō-ekō* is the cultivation of universal compassion towards all sentient beings coupled with the corresponding desire to save them from the lamentable bondage of this world. Rather than allow us to complacently fall into the belief that salvation is an end for ourselves alone, it promotes the idea of solidarity with all suffering creatures in samsāra. It also makes it meaningless to consider one's own salvation apart from that of all others for, ultimately, we all partake of the same spiritual 'substance'—Amida's infinite light and life.

If 'samsāra is Nirvāna', then the distressing plight of those who are suffering must, necessarily, be the profoundest concern of Amida Buddha whose sole reason for assuming 'name-and-form' (i.e., the *nembutsu*) was precisely for the sake of such beings. Nevertheless, the fact that we become bonded to Amida at death does not preclude us, as individuals here-and-now, from aspiring to save all beings once we are 'born' in the Pure Land. Such an attitude is inherent in the nature of compassion. But rather than returning as individual bodhisattvas, we 'return' as Amida, for we are none other than Amida in our pure state of Nirvāna. There is no need for a continual *gensō-ekō* as if to somehow 'supplement' the perfect saving power of Amida—because the Dharma-nature, in its oneness, accomplishes everything. In any case, the manifestations that one may assume (after having realised enlightenment) for the benefit of sentient beings in samsāra are, of course, endless. These manifestations, although giving the appearance of individual forms, are simply the myriad facets of Amida 'engaging' with the world of birth-and-death.

In the *Yuishinshō-mon'i*, Shinran states:

> Nirvāna is called 'extinction of passions', 'the uncreated', 'peaceful happiness', 'eternal bliss', 'true reality'. . . . We will unfailingly reach the Pure Land of happiness, whereupon we will be brought to realise the same enlightenment of great Nirvāna as Amida Tathāgata.

This is, indubitably, the final goal of all beings for *gensō-ekō* is surely not an end in itself. It is a means of bringing us all to the 'Great Nirvāna' without exception; and this is, precisely, what we attain in the Pure Land. In reality, however, it is Amida himself who perfectly fulfills *gensō-ekō*. In the Pure Land, any real distinction between Amida and those born there disappears because, in gaining birth, we shed our status as illusion-clad and passion-ridden creatures; we enter and become one with Amida's Infinite Light.* In fact, we could say that it is Amida's *gensō-ekō* that is continuous and unceasing, manifesting itself through the nembutsu and the saving power of shinjin. If Amida did not 'return' (in other words, become 'Dharma-Body as Compassion'), he would be merely 'Dharma-Body as Suchness' and thus remain forever unknowable.

It should be clear from what has already been said that, far from being an ineffectual allegory, the traditional notion of *gensō-ekō* pos-

---

* "Amida is a distinct personality from a samsaric standpoint but, from the Buddha's perspective, his personality is 'unhindered' and already involves every and all beings. It is only once our karmic debt has been exhausted by Amida, that this continuity can be realised." (Chris Morgan, *pers. comm.*)

sesses great spiritual and moral efficacy in its own right. It helps us to cultivate the proper attitude to our fellow creatures in conformity with the spirit of compassion, as well as acting as a salutary corrective to individualistic and narrow-minded tendencies in our spiritual aspirations. It is, indeed, a very vivid and moving way of reminding us of our profound spiritual bond with all beings, while helping to disseminate the much-needed spirit of Amida's compassion in our deeply troubled world. Although we may be unable to completely liberate others as we would wish, we can, at least, maintain this compassionate and merciful attitude to all those in misery, anguish and distress. This, in itself, is a fundamental way of sharing in Amida's compassionate embrace of the world. *Gensō-ekō* emphasises that our spiritual unity with others is never sundered—not even when we leave this world; and this in virtue of the all-pervasive and unhindered light of Amida Buddha that does not fail to penetrate and illumine even our darkest recesses.

Peace as Inner Transformation:
A Buddhist Perspective

> Overcome anger by peacefulness; overcome evil by good. Over-
> come the mean by generosity and the person who lies by truth.
>
> *The Dhammapada*[*]

In considering peace from a Buddhist perspective, it is important to
remember that it is, primarily, an inner disposition prior to its effective embodiment in the world as a particular course of action. Even
before this can be made possible, it must initially become the fruit of
spiritual realisation. This means that, in effect, any talk of peace
ought to be grounded in a vision of the spirit marked by wisdom,
compassion and equanimity.

> Our original Buddha-nature is ... omnipresent, silent and
> pure; it is a glorious and mysteriously peaceful joy.
>
> Huang Po[†]

This, in turn, naturally entails the recognition and practice of *ahimsa*,
a notion common to the Jains, Hindus, and Buddhists which prohib-
its the harming of sentient beings. This has always been regarded as
the cornerstone of any attempts to establish peace in the world among
these traditions. Without such a foundation, any practical initiatives
aimed at curtailing violence and upheaval in the world will waver, in
keeping with the fickle and unstable nature of unregenerate humanity. Of course, it may be objected that it is perfectly possible to aim for
peace on self-evident and purely humanitarian grounds without having recourse to religious justifications. Indeed there are numerous
worthy secular endeavours that seek to restore peace in our world,
albeit with limited success. Many such initiatives often involve a mix
of political strategies or appeals to self-interest in order to curtail the
suffering that is wrought on countless lives through the absence of
peaceful solutions to conflicts around the globe.

Peace on such terms is sure to be precarious if insufficiently
informed by deeper principles that involve *metanoia*, or a radical

---

[*] Juan Mascaro (tr.) *The Dhammapada: The Path of Perfection*, tr. (Harmond-
sworth: Penguin Books, 1983), p. 68.
[†] John Blofeld (tr.) *The Zen teaching of Huang Po* (New York: Grove Press, 1959),
p. 35.

change of heart. Now this is very difficult to achieve, even for those who profess to be adherents of religion (itself the cause of many bitter conflicts) which demonstrates, precisely, why peace is so elusive in our world. This difficulty also points to our troubled constitution as human beings and the countless 'blind passions' that afflict it; passions that are corrosive and inimical to any genuinely communal welfare:

> 'Blind passion' is a comprehensive term descriptive of all the forces, conscious and unconscious, that propel the unenlightened person to think, feel, act and speak in such a way as to cause uneasiness, frustration, torment and pain (mentally, emotionally, spiritually and even physically) for themselves and others. While Buddhism makes a detailed and subtle analysis of blind passion, employing such terms as craving, anger, delusion, arrogance, doubt and wrong views, fundamentally it is rooted in the fierce, stubborn clinging to the ... self that constitutes the basis of our existence. When we realise the full implications of this truth about ourselves, we see that the human condition is itself nothing but blind passion. Thus, just to live, or wanting to live, as an unenlightened being is to manifest blind passion at all times, regardless of what we may appear to be. One comes to know this, however, only through the illumination of great compassion.[*]

Considering the matter from Buddhist first principles, it is evident enough that true peace must reflect the serenity of Nirvāna as true reality, devoid of anger, hatred and ignorance.

> Nirvāna is called extinction of passions, the uncreated, peaceful happiness, eternal bliss, true reality.... Oneness and Buddhanature ... it fills the hearts and minds of all beings.
>
> Shinran[†]

It might seem an inordinate expectation to have peace in the world be contingent on the realisation of such an exalted state but, should this be a universal possibility for us, then the lasting peace which we so ardently seek would be secured by mere virtue of having attained

---

[*] *The Collected Works of Shinran*, tr. Dennis Hirota, Hisao Inagaki, Michio Tokunaga and Ryushin Uryuzu (Kyoto: Jōdo Shinshū Hongwanji-ha, 1997), vol. II, p. 172.
[†] *The Collected Works of Shinran*, tr. Dennis Hirota, Hisao Inagaki, Michio Tokunaga and Ryushin Uryuzu (Kyoto: Jōdo Shinshū Hongwanji-ha, 1997), vol. I, p. 461.

perfect enlightenment which conquers all opposition, division and conflict. However, in an age when Buddhism sees humanity as being subject to defilement and corruption, it must seem that the prospects for lasting peace look very bleak. 'Everything is burning' said the Buddha, 'burning with the fire of greed, with the fire of hatred, with the fire of delusion' (*Samyutta Nikāya*). The quenching of this fire is only possible through a profound spiritual transformation involving the irruption of wisdom and compassion into our lives—not through mere social service or political activism but by means of a far-reaching revolution in our ordinary consciousness that comes about when we encounter the light of the Buddha.

In this day and age, when attaining Buddhahood is considered largely impossible for ordinary people, it is left to us to simply take refuge in the Dharma and allow its liberating graces to lessen the hold that 'blind passions' have over us in our lives. This does not, of course, lead to any kind of personal perfection but it can attenuate the grip of illusion and discontent that is so often the harbinger of disorder in the world.

> Because they are deeply troubled and confused, people indulge their passions. Everyone is restlessly busy, having nothing on which to rely.... They entertain venomous thoughts, creating a widespread and dismal atmosphere of malevolence.... People are deluded by their passionate attachments, unaware of the Way, misguided and trapped by anger and enmity, and intent on gaining wealth and gratifying their desires like wolves.
> *Sūtra on the Buddha of Infinite Life**

The transcendent perspective afforded by our contact with nirvanic reality can, through contemplation and faith, steep us in the Buddhist virtues. This is none other than our encounter with the Absolute:

> We are told that Nirvana is permanent, stable, imperishable, immovable, ageless, deathless and unborn; that it is power, bliss and happiness, the secure refuge, the shelter and the place of unassailable safety; that it is the real Truth and the supreme Reality; that it is the Good, the supreme goal and the one and

---

* Hisao Inagaki (tr.), *The Three Pure Land Sūtras* (Kyoto: Nagata Bunshodo, 2000), p. 286.

only consummation of our life—the eternal, hidden and incomprehensible Peace.

Edward Conze[*]

In a sense, we need to become channels for this spiritual force in order that our hearts may be transformed. Without this, no lasting peace of any kind is possible seeing as the outer world of human affairs can only be a reflection of what is taking place within us. In the absence of a revealed religious law in Buddhism—such as we find in some of the Semitic traditions—the Mahāyāna, for example, advocates observance of the 'Six Perfections', or *pāramitās*, as the basis of spiritual and ethical endeavour. These comprise: *dāna* (generosity, giving of oneself); *sīla* (virtue, morality, discipline, proper conduct); *ksānti* (patience, tolerance, forbearance, acceptance, endurance); *vīrya* (energy, diligence, vigor, effort); *dhyāna* (contemplation, concentration); and *prajñā* (wisdom, insight).

Many of those who adhere to a religiously fundamentalist mind-set appear to lack an adequate understanding of the basic tenets of their faith or willfully ignore them for ideological reasons. This can only be addressed effectively by a proper presentation of the teachings in a balanced and nuanced manner. The contradictions and betrayals one often finds in fundamentalist thought often reflect a lack of intellectual depth and sophistication or an insistence on simplistic solutions in the face of complex problems. This might be understandable if the motive was compassion or *ahimsa* but, almost always, these aberrations are impelled by a disturbed religious psyche and therefore quite pernicious.

The Buddhist faith has sometimes been criticised for being too flexible when it comes to its doctrinal pronouncements; a fact which has spawned a plethora of different schools and teachings which often appear to contradict each other. While this bewildering variety of perspectives can seem confusing to newcomers, it may also be considered as one of its hidden strengths and the reason why Buddhism has largely avoided religious conflicts on the scale seen in some other

---

[*] Edward Conze, *Buddhism: Its Essence and Development* (New York: Harper & Row, 1975), p. 40.

faiths.* Traditionally, the Buddha is said to have given '84,000' different teachings in response to the almost limitless variety of human needs, temperaments and understanding yet with always the same objective in mind:

> The Buddha aspires to benefit sentient beings by giving them . . . a great realm of ultimate purity, peace and sustenance.
>
> Zonkaku†

This diversity does not suggest that there is no 'bedrock' in its teachings but, rather, that there are a core set of key insights which subtly tie together the variegated threads of the Dharma. Adherence to them is not necessarily insisted upon as a dogmatic requirement but is a natural outcome of reflecting on the truths of human existence. This latitude in belief acts as a foil to fundamentalism in that it reveals the incompleteness or relativity of any single doctrinal standpoint, while stressing that each one is perfectly adequate as a vehicle for emancipation. In this way, the range of teachings available in Buddhism can be seen as complementary rather than competing, thus removing the sclerotic tendency to form fixed and definitive views on spiritual matters—a major source of religious conflict.

This means that we ought to acknowledge that any doctrinal formulation is only an approximation of a reality that transcends it and

---

* Nevertheless, one cannot overlook the serious episodes of violent behaviour that have afflicted Buddhism throughout its history. Recent examples include the attacks against Muslims undertaken at the behest of nationalist monks in Thailand (2004), Burma (2013) and Sri Lanka (2014). In 1998, thousands of monks of the Chogye Buddhist order in South Korea fought each other in protracted pitched battles, vying for control of the order's considerable wealth and property. In the 1970s, ethnic Lao Buddhist monks actively supported militant violence directed against the country's communists. One can also point to the support given by a number of prominent Buddhist authorities for Japan's militarisation during the second world war as well as the assassination plot, known as 'The League of Blood' incident in 1932, which was led by a Buddhist monk. Numerous violent episodes have also been documented in the history of Tibetan Buddhism where competing sects have engaged in brutal clashes and summary executions over hundreds of years.

† Alfred Bloom (ed.), *The Shin Buddhist Classical Tradition: A Reader in Pure Land Teaching* (*Volume 1*), (Bloomington: World Wisdom, 2013), p. 119.

which must always remain an ineffable experience of the spirit. Doing so does not belittle the teachings as being only 'half-true', so to speak, such as to vitiate their efficacy. On the contrary, this is assured by their having emerged from the realm of truth and light revealed to the Buddha in his enlightenment experience.

> The Buddha regards universal existence with detached Wisdom and impartial Compassion. The aim of his teaching and method is liberation from all partial and illusory viewpoints, coloured by desire and aversion, into a state of peace and well-being.
>
> Harold Stewart[*]

When awakened to Nirvāna, the Buddha recognised the truth of human existence coupled with a liberating awareness granted by such truth. Any articulation of this sublime vision is, inevitably, a descent from a perfect apprehension of a non-verbal wholeness to a more fragmentary and imperfect recourse to everyday language; language which, nevertheless, points to the source of its meaning and— if rightly apprehended—to the same unitive experience that forms the fount of all doctrine.

Accordingly, the Buddhist solution to the problem of fundamentalism, from which other traditions may gain a useful perspective, is to see dogma as supple and diaphanous; something that still captures the profoundest insights of a spiritual tradition but which, nonetheless, does not fix them into a rigid or inflexible posture. This enables us to see the symbolic and allegorical nature of sacred texts rather than being bound by a suffocating literalism that confuses truth with a 'dead letter'. Such an approach admittedly contains risks for those to whom such a balance is either too elusive or an outright threat to 'black and white' doctrinairism. This, in turn, can provoke either an arrogant and overly self-assured fundamentalism that is fatal to the spiritual life or to a type of vague sentimentalism lacking in both insight and rigour; both of which may lead to a loss of belief altogether through having been starved of genuine contact with the living sources of religion.

---

[*] Harold Stewart, *By the Old Walls of Kyoto: A Year's Cycle of Landscape Poems with Prose Commentaries* (New York: Weatherhill, 1981), p. 152.

Given the irreconcilable positions of the secular and religious outlooks, it is difficult to effect any kind of harmony at a spiritual level. However, there are insights furnished by some Eastern traditions that ought to lend themselves to universal acceptance; for example, the notion of *ahimsa*, as has already been mentioned. Non-believers would argue that religions do not have a monopoly on this concept (which, indeed, they have often flouted) but, nevertheless, it is an important point of convergence given that the most egregious manifestations of religious intolerance have been widespread violence and harm done to others. Both from a secular point of view and a spiritual one, it is difficult to dispute the primacy of *ahimsa* as a preliminary step in securing a united response against the destructive forces of terrorism and nihilism.

It is important to explain why the truth of *ahimsa* goes to the heart of the difference between a sacred and a profane attitude to reality. In Mahāyāna Buddhism (and of course one sees this in other traditions as well), the empirical world around us, and the sentient beings that are central to it, comprise a manifestation of the highest reality considered as either Nirvāna or the Dharma-Body.

In light of the above, this reality and the world must stand in a relationship of non-duality. As a further consequence, this entails that each manifested entity (natural, animal or human) is strictly interdependent with all others, regardless of how evident this may be to our ordinary perception. Therefore, in causing harm to others, we injure ourselves as we are thereby inflicting pain and suffering on the whole which then recoils upon us as an integral part of that whole. Similarly—though less obviously—any harm we do to ourselves can also be correspondingly detrimental to other beings. Such a scission in the fabric of the world—while unavoidable given its imperfection and impermanence—can deny us the beneficent influence of Nirvāna which aims to unify all beings and save them from the acute perils of pain and ignorance.

> May I, and other aspirants, behold the Buddha, acquire the eye of non-defilement, be born in the Land of Peace and Bliss, and realise the supreme enlightenment.
>
> Shan-tao[*]

[*] Alfred Bloom (ed.), *The Shin Buddhist Classical Tradition: A Reader in Pure Land Teaching* (*Volume 2*), (Bloomington: World Wisdom, 2014), p. 24.

This account of the metaphysical basis for compassion and the accompanying attitude of *ahimsa*, to which it gives rise, is evidently a deeper explanation than what a merely secular view is able to provide. This does not mean that the latter cannot be sincerely felt and passionately defended but it does suggest that a more profound understanding of why *ahimsa* must be true is usually absent. To be fair, however, many religious defenders of this perspective themselves often fail to comprehend it properly or, worse, pervert it for less than spiritual motives.

That said, common ground is still possible based on a shared understanding of *ahimsa* as an indispensable principle of peace-building in our broken world. While the reasons for accepting the imperative to avoid harming others may not always be the same, a unanimous agreement as to the necessity of such a principle is surely possible among people of good will, discernment and sensitivity, regardless of religious belief.

It remains a challenge for religions to be a catalyst in the promotion of peace and harmony when they have often been responsible for much hatred and conflict. Yet, as already mentioned, concepts such as the harmony of all beings in the Absolute and the interconnectedness of reality can serve as a means to have traditional spirituality and ethics contribute to a deeper grasp of our existential plight. They also suggest ways in which the many horrors of fundamentalist violence can be attenuated through a penetrating awareness of the twin Buddhist virtues of wisdom and compassion—the only true and enduring remedy for conflict borne of 'blind passion'.

In suggesting the above, one must not be carried away by a false sense of optimism. While some of these suggested solutions are correct in principle, their effective realisation appears to be an objective well out of reach. A number of religions prescribe to the idea that we are living in a period of spiritual degradation the likes of which are arguably unprecedented. For the Hindus, we are in the midst of the 'Age of Kali' and many Buddhists consider that we find ourselves in the 'Decadent Age of the Dharma':

> At the horrible time of the end, men will be malevolent, false, wicked and obtuse and they will imagine that they have reached perfection when it will be nothing of the sort.
>
> *Lotus Sūtra**

Conflict and turmoil are seen as an inherent aspect of such an age and, as distressing as such developments are, they are to be expected and one ought not to anticipate dramatic improvements any time soon. While our ability to collectively redress this crisis may be seriously limited, we can at least aim at working on our own inner spiritual disposition (and helping others to do so) without which nothing positive can emerge in world affairs. The state of disorder that we see around us everywhere is a reflection of a toxic or damaged consciousness which only a spiritual form of awakening can ameliorate. Failing such a possibility in this life, Buddhism and other faiths exhort us to seek solace in the prospect of an eschatological resolution to the evils that can never be fully overcome in our fractured existence.

> This world is a place full of disagreeable affairs, stealing, war, anger, hunger, desire. But the other shore is Nirvāna, beyond karma; it is true peace, freedom and happiness so, naturally, we look for the Other Shore. . . . In this world, we cannot obtain true freedom—there are always obstructions. Our life is temporary, not permanent, and we do not have true peace.
>
> Hozen Seki†

While the secular world may not accept this diagnosis, it needs to keep an open mind as to the validity of this truth, especially given the worsening deterioration in our moral and social ambience. The solution to this impasse can never be a political one alone—ultimately, it must be buttressed by a spiritual dimension. Politics can certainly deliver on compromises or half-measures but the underlying impetus has to be an ethical orientation that is illumined through an encounter with a transcendent order of reality, on which every genuine value is based. Even at this level, sectarian differences should not preclude the attempt to seek an essential shared understanding. It is therefore important to look beyond certain doctrinal differences to a vision that is truly communal and to which all the great faiths can

---

* John Paraskevopoulos (ed.), *The Fragrance of Light: A Journey Into Buddhist Wisdom* (Sophia Perennis, 2015), p. 32.
† Hozen Seki, *The Great Natural Way* (New York: American Buddhist Academy, 1976), p. 73.

assent—a joint attempt to affirm peace in the world that is none other than a peace that reflects, for Buddhists at least, the beatitude of Nirvāna that lies at the heart of reality and which seeks to bring all beings to the highest good.

Whether we can ascend to such an exalted realisation remains highly uncertain. If we prove that we are unable to do so, what can be assured is the slow but inevitable disintegration of human dignity and the abandonment of its most noble ideals.

> 'Wherever the Buddha comes to stay, there is no state, town or village that is not blessed by his virtues. The whole country reposes in peace and harmony. The sun and the moon shine with pure brilliance; winds rise and rains fall at the right time. There is no calamity or epidemic and so the country becomes wealthy, and its people enjoy peace. Soldiers and weapons become useless; and people esteem virtue, practise benevolence and diligently cultivate courteous modesty'.... The Buddha continued, 'But after I have departed from this world, my teaching will gradually decline and people will fall prey to flattery and deceit, and commit various evils.'
>
> *Sūtra on the Buddha of Immeasurable Life**

---

* Hisao Inagaki (tr.), *The Three Pure Land Sūtras* (Kyoto: Nagata Bunshodo, 2000), p.304.

The more the mind wishes for eternity, the more it feels pain and suffering. That is the exact reason that there is a path to clear the pain and suffering.

Haya Akegarasu

PART FOUR

Miscellaneous

Interview with Greek Journal, Avaton

Shin Buddhism is little known in the West. Can you tell us, in a few words, how it developed and how it differs from the classical form of Buddhism which most people recognise?

Shin Buddhism is still largely unknown in the West although the situation has improved markedly in the past 10-15 years thanks to numerous internet sites devoted to this tradition. Today, Shin is the largest form of Buddhism in Japan (a fact which may surprise many given the far greater prominence given to schools such as Zen). Its teachings have their origins in India and were developed by a number of masters, both in that country, as well as in China and Japan. It represents the Buddha's teaching for ordinary lay people who are unable to live a monastic life, practise effective meditation or undergo ascetic disciplines. For this reason, and also because it is aimed at people who live busy and distracted lives in a tumultuous world of endless troubles and uncertainty, I believe it to be the most accessible and compassionate of Buddhist doctrines. It is also, in light of the actual capabilities of ordinary people, the most realistic.

What is the basic message, the central truth, that Shin Buddhism brings to modern people?

The principal message of Shin Buddhism is to make known the unconditional compassion that is extended to all sentient beings by Amida, Buddha of Immeasurable Light and Boundless Life. This is the ultimate reality that pervades all existence but which also transcends its limitations and imperfections. It is essentially one with Nirvāna which is the emancipation from all suffering. Amida, as the *Infinite*, represents the personified face of this reality—the aspect that is presented to suffering humanity in its quest for spiritual liberation. You might wonder how this differs from conventional notions of God in theistic traditions. Without getting into all of the subtleties involved, one can say that Amida Buddha is not a 'judge' but, rather, represents absolute compassion which does not punish or condemn any transgressions. This Buddha has effectively vowed to rescue all beings, from the 'burning house' of this life, who simply entrust themselves to his saving power. Nothing further is required of believers—as finite and bounded creatures, we are capable of little else other than surrendering to this Light. Another difference is that Amida Buddha is not the 'creator' of the universe in the sense that is commonly understood. The world is not 'willed' into existence by a being that stands apart from us. Our existence is seen as a manifestation of an ultimate reality that seeks to have us return to it. It is not an all-powerful deity that can do anything (hence there is no 'problem of evil' in the Christian sense) but because conditioned existence arises from it in a spontaneous, natural but limited manner, everything is interconnected and, in wishing to save all beings, Amida Buddha is actually saving aspects of himself which have become lost in a fragmented world of impermanence and suffering. Therefore, the Oneness of all things, and the Compassion at the heart of reality, guarantees our eventual emancipation from the unsatisfactory snares of life which, in the end, are only ephemeral (regardless of how real they may seem to us now).

There is a widespread view that, to follow a spiritual path, one's everyday life needs to be relatively manageable without any particular problems. How true is this?

Shin Buddhism has a unique approach to spiritual practice. It states, quite explicitly, that there is no practice that we—as flawed mortals—can undertake in order to rid ourselves of our fallibilities. Buddhism speaks of the 'blind passions' of ignorance, greed and anger that plague our lives. As long as we remain unenlightened beings, we cannot eradicate the profound limitations of our earthly existence. In many ways, the power of the ego is central to Shin's assessment of human reality and it concludes that egocentric behaviour in us is so powerful and all-consuming, that it cannot be vanquished by this very same ego doing something concrete to free itself. Even many advanced practitioners of meditation today (including some of those who consider themselves 'masters') have failed to eliminate the poison of egoism within themselves. In this sense, all beings are broken, confused and brittle. Shin Buddhism says that, in order to overcome our perilous existential condition, we need to rely on the power of the Buddha which is not subject to these imperfections. This is also known as 'Other-Power' in contrast to the narrow and limited efficacy of our own 'self-power'. True practice, therefore, can only be undertaken by the Buddha on our behalf if we let it pervade our hearts and minds.

Miscellaneous

We live in a troubled world characterised by uncertainty, especially in Greece during recent times. People live in trepidation today and fear tomorrow even more. What can one do to address the fears that breed in our hearts in such situations?

The Buddha taught that fear and uncertainty are the chief hallmarks of human existence in this life. A world such as ours, which is incomplete and so full of shortcomings, cannot be otherwise and we, to the extent that we identify ourselves entirely with it as unenlightened beings, will always suffer accordingly. In fact, the crisis in Greece at the moment is a salutary reminder of how unpredictable life can be, given that so many of our fundamental desires are extremely difficult (perhaps even impossible) to fulfill under such conditions. So, while the numerous anxieties, problems and difficulties in our lives cannot be eliminated, there are things we can do to lessen the impact of our suffering. Observing the basic Buddhist virtues such as wisdom, kindness, generosity, love, sympathy and selflessness, can go a long way towards decreasing much of the grief that people inflict on each other. We may not always be able to practise such virtues perfectly but modest efforts towards curbing the insatiable urges of our dark egos will help us to live as human beings, as best as we can, rather than living beneath ourselves. As for the ravages and destruction wrought by natural or economic disasters, we must also remember another important lesson from the Buddha; namely, that all life is ephemeral. Accordingly, many of the desirable things that it seems to offer should be seen in light of our ultimate good which is enlightenment to true wisdom and compassion, as well as freedom from the oppressive round of 'birth-and-death' (*samsāra*). In other words, becoming awakened to this highest reality places all things in their correct perspective and lessens our attachments (human as they doubtlessly are) to the things that are perishable (including, of course, our own lives).

Why do we suffer? Is there an antidote?

As indicated above, we suffer because we often mis-identify our true good and harbour misplaced notions of what constitutes our genuine well-being. So much of what we pursue in everyday life is bound to let us down, sooner or later, because it is precariously unstable and thus cannot be relied on to confer true happiness. The world is constantly changing—nothing remains the same—so becoming invested in worldly objectives, as ends in themselves, is guaranteed to lead to disappointment because they lack permanence and do not satisfy our real needs (of which we are often oblivious). The 'antidote' is a greater adherence to spiritual goods which do not fade with time and which are not affected by the uncertainties of existence. As our true nature is spiritual, and not confined to the restrictions of this world, our pursuit should, primarily, be of those things that fulfill our deepest nature.

What are the first steps that one can take in order to lighten the emotional weight that we feel in the face of life's difficulties?

While the Buddhist path is distinguished by its teaching of great compassion, we must not forget that it is also a path of *wisdom*. Even if someone is not particularly spiritual, a simple and dispassionate observation of the realities of everyday life should lead them to conclude that there is something very wrong with our situation in this world. The first step, therefore, is to realise what the Buddha taught as the 'First Noble Truth'—the very basis of his teaching. To understand that human suffering and dissatisfaction is universal naturally leads us to want to overcome it. With time and careful attention to this great truth, we gradually awaken to the fact that the solution to the problem of the world cannot be found *within* the world. We must look beyond it, consistent with our profoundest longings, in order to discover that our salvation lies in a realm that surpasses this world of suffering and impermanence—the eternal realm of Dharma, Nirvāna and Enlightenment which we can encounter even now.

One of the main causes of our unhappiness, according to Buddhism, is our attachment to earthly things as well as to life's pleasures. But pleasures are a basic component of life, as is the need that one feels for a higher reality. Can these two aspects coexist in our lives?

As ordinary beings, our attachment to the pleasures, comforts and consolations of this life are natural and inevitable. They are not to be condemned unless they become excessive and therefore the cause of harm to oneself or others. This is what the Buddha warns us against. By becoming too preoccupied with our attachments, and the passing fashions of this world, we risk overlooking the true remedy to our existential sickness, which is the Dharma. Being human, we must be permitted those things that make our everyday existence bearable while, at the same time, not depending on them too much for our ultimate happiness—something which they cannot possibly give. We must learn to balance the requirements of our hearts and our bodies with the deeper needs of the spirit. The latter puts the former in perspective and the former allows us to pursue the latter in a balanced and human manner. As embodied creatures, we are subject to a host of perils, diseases and tragedies. We can do our best to avoid them or lessen their impact but, in the end, they are unavoidable. It is perfectly understandable that we are a liable to become attached to loved ones, our homes, possessions, lifestyles, economic security, and so forth, but we must not depend on them. Having a spiritual focus helps us to put everything in its proper place and to lessen the shock of losing those very things which never really belong to us in the first place. There can be no surer proof that our true home must lie elsewhere—in Amida's 'Pure Land' of limitless Light and Life—the traces of which we can find here, even in our crepuscular world, wherever we nurture goodness, love, truth and beauty.

You have mentioned the importance of beauty, recalling the famous phrase of Dostoevsky, 'Beauty will save the world'. How do you understand this and experience it in your life? How can one impart beauty to our everyday lives?

Yes, beauty is very important in restoring the sense of the sacred in our everyday lives. Of course, many think that beauty is just a subjective response to certain things we enjoy or admire in the world; simply a matter of 'taste' without reference to anything objective. I believe this is a very narrow attitude to have and one that is, in any case, quite false. Qualities like love and beauty are very accessible to us all, even if we do not have a spiritual perspective on life. However, all the great religious traditions of humanity teach that these qualities have a spiritual origin which can help us to glimpse something of this higher world that, in Buddhism, we know as Nirvāna. Because the essence of this reality is bliss, it takes form in our world as those experiences in life that give us a foretaste of it. Beauty and love, of course, are among the most powerful of these, even though they may be imperfectly realised in this life. They have a transcendent quality, our attraction to which helps us to rise above ourselves and our petty concerns. They also prompt us to lead lives of gratitude and generosity in that we wish to give freely to others those blessings which we have received ourselves in our encounter with the sublime and beautiful things of this world. The Buddhist master Kūkai once said: "Everything that is beautiful partakes of the Buddha." By cultivating the seed of beauty wherever we can, despite the prevalence of so much harsh ugliness in the world, we open a door to the Buddha's light which can then shine through and dispel our hardness of heart. This will make our lives more transparent to that supreme reality which is the seat of imperishable beauty and the source of everything we love and treasure in this life.

[Published in *Avaton* (Issue No. 141, October–November 2015) and translated into Greek by Petros Theodorides]

Preface to the Italian edition of
The Larger Sūtra on Immeasurable Life

This sūtra speaks to our fundamental condition and our ultimate hopes. It is a sacred text that has been an inspiration for millions of people for centuries and which, even to this day, continues to give deep comfort and joy to those who find themselves bewildered by our world of suffering. Why has it been so popular? A cursory glance at its contents may not necessarily demonstrate the reason. Initially, especially if one has not encountered this kind of text before, one may be overwhelmed by the fantastic scale of its descriptions, the extraordinary imagination at work, the cosmic timescales involved and the almost surreal ambience that it creates.

Beneath all the rich imagery, profound symbolism and unfathomable mysteries of the great salvific drama contained in this sūtra, lies a very simple and powerful message. Its fundamental insight is to declare the compassionate nature of ultimate reality which embraces all sentient beings without exception. This reality is expressed in the most exalted terms—Infinite Light and Endless Life—and is embodied in that great object of veneration which has given succour to countless devotees over many centuries: Amida Buddha and his Land of Utmost Bliss. It is not important whether you take these as literal realities 'out there' or as ways of describing, in more accessible terms, profound Buddhist notions such as Nirvāna or Suchness—the core truth remains the same. This ineffable reality, which comprises the highest Wisdom and Compassion, lies within all things and has vowed to have us return to it—a realm of inconceivable happiness, where we truly belong, and to which we are called by Amida Buddha through his Name—*Namo Amida Butsu*. Our response to this call, with joyful faith, is the awakening that takes place when the Buddha penetrates our cold ego and shines into our hearts. Such an encounter can demonstrate the truth of this reality and its compassionate working, as well as being the source of inspiration that impels us to share this splendid teaching with others.

While it is easy to be cynical about the claims of this scripture and to dismiss its insights as the feeble longings of a deluded mind, this would be a very grave mistake. The only response to such corrosive scepticism is to experience directly the transforming encounter which the text promises to all who abandon their aimless, painful, self-absorbed and—ultimately—futile attempts at realising enduring worldly happiness and fulfillment. We can only gain our true self when we abandon our false one, which we habitually take as the only reality there is. The heart of this wonderful message—religion in its purest form—is that Amida Buddha seeks to emancipate all beings from their heavy weight of karma and that this is made possible by simply abandoning ourselves to the compassionate embrace that is offered to us unconditionally. The sūtra tells us this, and more, in glorious, uplifting and unforgettable language that will continue to inspire and nourish future generations of genuine seekers who long for true answers to the deepest questions of life and death.

[Published in *I Sutra della Terra Pura, Vol. 2* (Myo Edizioni, 2015) and translated into Italian by Massimo Claus & Laura Silvestri]

The 35th Vow

> If, when I attain Buddhahood, women in the immeasurable and inconceivable Buddha-lands of the ten quarters who, having heard my Name, rejoice in faith, awaken aspiration for Enlightenment and wish to renounce womanhood, should after death be reborn again as women, may I not attain perfect Enlightenment.

The 35th Vow from the *Larger Sūtra on Immeasurable Life* has been the subject of much controversy, as well as consternation, as it appears to reflect an unfavourable attitude towards women. However, this is certainly not the case. Essentially, it was a compassionate teaching for female aspirants living at a time (presumably second or third century India) when life for women would have been a largely dreadful affair. One can only imagine that the suffering of so many women then was such that a great number of them would have no doubt wished for rebirth as a man in any subsequent existence in order to avoid the miseries of their lot in life. Indeed, there is evidence in some writings that many women despised their condition and may have thought that their birth in a female form was some kind of karmic retribution. So, even in the eyes of many women themselves, there would have been a view that being female was something unfortunate from which they would want to seek release. If this is correct, then to hear the Buddha vow that women in the present world can attain birth in the Pure Land where there are no 'beings in the female form', might well have seemed a most liberating (indeed an almost impossible to believe) teaching that offered the only lasting release from their deplorable social condition. Now, obviously, there are no biological sexes in the Pure Land but, from the point of view of rousing the aspiration of female devotees to attain enlightenment, the Buddha used an *upāya* or 'saving means' to encourage them in their faith. The teaching was therefore tailored to the conditions in which most women found themselves, even if it meant having to take into account the prejudices of the time in order to do so.

This situation was compounded by the fact that progress on any kind of spiritual path was barred for many women and one recalls the difficulty and resistance the Buddha faced in establishing an order for nuns. In that light, the only hope that the great majority of women had was to attain birth in a realm where their sex was no longer going to be a problem for them. Indeed, the Buddha's 4th Vow states: "If, when I attain Buddhahood, humans and devas in my land should not all be of *one appearance*, and should there be any difference in beauty, may I not attain perfect Enlightenment." But rather than talk about a non-dual realm of sexless existence (probably a difficult and abstract concept for most ordinary folk at the time), it was more tangible to speak of no longer possessing a female form (seeing as it had such negative implications for women themselves) or even attaining a male one (given the spiritual privileges that were afforded to men) so that this would have been a very powerful incentive for women to follow the Pure Land path. It is not that the Dharma has bought into, or reflects, a misogynistic perspective in itself but rather that it needed to accommodate itself to the discrimination prevalent at the time in order to address the plight of everyday women in terrible situations.

If a woman during that period of history was told that being female posed no impediment to attaining everlasting bliss in the Pure Land (thus never having to suffer from those disadvantages again) and that there was nothing to do except entrust in the Buddha's Vow, she would doubtlessly be overcome by immense joy and spiritual relief, especially seeing as there would be no other option for someone like her. No doubt, a modern woman would look at a Vow like that and be appalled but, in pre-feminist patriarchal India, it would have surely raised the spirits of countless women and given them genuine hope for salvation.

Excerpts from Pastoral Counsel

(a) *Questions from a correspondent*

Q: I have been very drawn, in my readings over the years, to Pure Land literature though not to the traditional doctrinal and mythological language or to conventional practices.

I am intrigued to hear you say this. You need to identify exactly what it is that attracts you to Pure Land Buddhism because, if you strip away 'traditional doctrinal and mythological language' you are not left with very much. It is unfortunate that the symbolism of the Pure Land teachings is a deterrent to you. Each spiritual tradition needs to be clothed in some form or other. No one can perceive ultimate reality as it really is given that its nature is, literally, inconceivable. If it did not disclose itself in intelligible forms, no one would know anything about it. Accordingly, the Pure Land tradition has embodied its teachings in a certain 'mythological' guise in order to make the aspiration for Enlightenment and Nirvāna easier for ordinary people. It tries to employ imagery from our known world to suggest the highest bliss in terms that we can understand. These images need not be taken literally but they can be used as a springboard to approach this reality (and everyone needs training wheels to start with!).

Q: Sitting zazen, with the premium it places on 'the longer one sits the better', has always left me unfulfilled. A sense of grace is not present. It simply has not worked for me. I do seem to have a 'heart' connection to Pure Land (but unfortunately not to the conventional language and practice). I am really on my own without a sangha to relate to. I read and practise by myself but not out of choice. What is your feeling about my sitting in zazen with others while possibly trying visualisation as well as reciting the nembutsu as much as I can in the hope of deepening my shinjin?

A feeling of isolation, among those interested in Shin, is a common experience for many people in Western countries. If you feel that you cannot entirely divorce yourself from *zazen* practice then, by all means, continue to recite the nembutsu while sitting with others or attempt visualisation according to the *Contemplation Sūtra* if you are capable of it. You cannot force *shinjin*—it will come of itself when you are ready. Therefore, you should not recite the nembutsu with a view to fabricating this experience for yourself or expecting some immediate benefit. It can only be conferred by Amida. All you can do is patiently remain open to the Buddha's influence while deepening your 'hearing' of the Dharma. Nembutsu practice should be done in a spirit of openness and mindfulness of the Buddha—Amida can take better care of your shinjin than you ever will. The very fact that you are drawn to the Pure Land way, in the first place, is a sign that Amida is already working within you.

Q: I once went to a Pure Land temple a number of years ago and did not see the 'Sunday service' style as a good fit. What is your opinion?

The temple can be helpful in providing you with a focus for hearing the dharma and discussing your faith with others. In that respect, the sangha is very important. I can certainly understand that the services may not meet your needs in every respect but you may find that other members may prove a valuable resource to you. However, regular attendance at a temple is by no means obligatory. One's priority should be awakening to Amida's mind; something that can occur at any place and at any time.

Q: Can you say something about how Amida is the personification of the Absolute and the nembutsu as its form? I get stuck on the strictly mythological arguments but would love to deepen my realisation and belief in those.

You should not be overly concerned with the 'mythological arguments', especially when you realise what they are trying to do ("Myth embodies the nearest approach to absolute truth that can be stated in words"—Ananda Coomaraswamy). As I mentioned earlier, ultimate reality—which is formless—needs to adopt a form in order to communicate with sentient beings. To do this, it assumes the aspect of Amida Buddha, the Pure Land, *shinjin* and the *nembutsu.* There is no way we can assimilate the Shin experience and teachings other than through such means. Amida has provided us with these precisely for this reason, so that we may know the Buddha and become free from our spiritual blindness. The Absolute as *Dharmakāya* is 'supra-personal' in the sense that it transcends mere human personality but it is by no means impersonal. It is greater than anything we can understand as conventional personality and is the source of all value that we find in it. Nevertheless, the Dharmakāya manifests a personal form in the reality of Amida so that it may impart its wisdom and compassion to us. Indeed, it is this very compassion that impels Amida to descend from the heights of inconceivability and reach out to suffering humanity in a guise to which we can easily respond. The forms it takes are not ultimate reality in themselves—they simply serve as a means (though indispensable means) by which we can realise shinjin and, ultimately, attain Nirvāna.

Q: You have stated that 'Amida dwells at the core of our despair and anxiety—indeed these very circumstances often provide the most powerful opportunities for the disclosure of his compassion'. Why does Amida dwell in our despair and anxiety? It is very encouraging and hopeful, especially for a deluded person like myself, to think that Amida is there for me.

Being all-pervading, Amida is ubiquitous in every situation in which we find ourselves. However, it is usually when we are at 'rock bottom', in states of anxiety and despair, that we are more inclined to be receptive to this presence. When we are vulnerable, confused or scared, we find that the things on which we usually rely in life can let us down or be incapable of providing the answers we are looking for. In these instances, we cease to depend on everyday reality for spiritual comfort and cast our gaze at Amida, from whom we seek refuge and illumination. Therefore, it is not that the Buddha dwells particularly in despair (he also dwells in our moments of joy)—only that it is on such occasions that we can sense his presence more deeply as all our usual supports gradually come to be taken away, leaving us with little else in which to trust. Therefore, when we invoke *Namo Amida Butsu* we are saying "I take *refuge* in the Infinite'. Shinjin is when we say this and *mean* it.

(b) *Response to a correspondent*

I do not want to deny, for a moment, that all the great schools of the Mahāyāna share much in common—however, there remain important differences which is why they went their separate ways (and also why it is very difficult to isolate what constitutes 'quintessential' Mahāyāna).

You say that it 'is their opposing claims that sets them apart from others, creating an atmosphere of contention and competition (e.g. Jōdo Shinshū vs. Zen)'. Each of these 'claims' encapsulates an aspect of the truth and the diversity of such claims reflects the complex variation found in human needs, mentalities, dispositions, capabilities and imagination—otherwise they would not exist. Under such conditions, competition or conflict is inevitable. However, the fact that they are relative does not imply that they are not effective. Forms and symbols are very important. If they seem limited, it is only because they address themselves to limited beings. Suchness is able to manifest itself in an inexhaustible variety of forms in order to reach out to us. However, since 'form is emptiness and emptiness is form' the power of Suchness to awaken us through such means is not restricted by this apparent limitation (for it only appears so from our perspective).

For example, the Name of Amida Buddha is considered to be one with the Buddha's reality. In other words, although the Name takes a particular form, it is still a vehicle for the highest truth as it is actually the form assumed by Suchness itself—Enlightenment 'in action'. It is not as if one is dealing with an inferior mode of this reality. From the perspective of the Absolute, forms are empty and do not constitute a barrier to its omnipresent action in samsāra (which is, in itself, an unreal notion from the side of tathatā). But we must walk before we can run, hence the endless gradations of spiritual awakening afforded by the innumerable *upāyas* displayed by the Tathāgata according to each person's need and capacity—all of these saving means will ultimately lead to the absolute truth (which is, after all, their reason for being) because they are grounded in Suchness and are none other than Suchness in active mode.

(c) *Questions from a correspondent* (*Part 2*)

Q: What form can the nembutsu take? I assume that the essential element is 'Amida' or 'Amitābha'. Do the six characters of the nembutsu in Shin have special significance beyond the Name? Have you heard of Shin Buddhists simply invoking 'Amida' directly? Would it be considered disrespectful to do so?

I was quite interested in this question many years ago and wrote to a number of teachers about it. One of them told me that the way you

said it was not that important because the Name, in essence, is formless. I did not think this was a very satisfactory response seeing as a
name—by definition—is clearly a form and engaged with as such. At
the other end of the spectrum, the emphatic view of one Japanese
scholar (representing the traditional position) was that, although the
Buddha's Name is *Amida/Amitābha*, the nembutsu as invoked must
include *Namo* as well, since this constitutes the all-important act of
taking refuge on our part. The six-character *myōgō* is the standard
formulation and the one most commonly used (notwithstanding its
various contracted forms) but there are also longer variations which
are also quite traditional: (i) the ten-character name, *Kimyō Jinjippō
Mugekō Nyōrai* ('I take refuge in the Tathāgata of Light Unhindered
in the Ten Quarters'); and (ii) the nine-character name, *Namo
Fukashigikō Nyōrai* ('I take refuge in the Tathāgata of Inconceivable
Light'). This form also appears, less commonly, as the eight-charac-
ter name, *Namo Fukashigikō Butsu*.

As you can see, *Namo* or *Kimyō* (in its Sino-Japanese form) is considered an integral part of the invocation. However, I have observed that
some Chinese Pure Land groups simply say *Amito-fo*, including when
greeting or farewelling people. Therefore, I do not believe that it is
'disrespectful' to simply say 'Amida' but it just seems to go against the
grain of the tradition itself which prefers to see the nembutsu as the
coming together of us and the Buddha (in the act of invocation) as
well as the dependence of the former on the latter through the use of
Namo. This was very prominent in Rennyo's notion of *kihō ittai*—the
unity of the devotee and Amida Buddha.

Over the years, some people have asked me if it is acceptable to say
the nembutsu in other than the main canonical languages of San-
skrit, Chinese and Japanese. I am not aware of any *nembutsu* forms
in Western languages but it is perfectly fine to say it in English, for
example, if one feels so inclined. However, I find that it is a little
more cumbersome in that form and seems to lack a certain sacred
resonance.

*Q: I have been reading 'The Shin Buddhist Classical Tradition' and
some of the traditional texts quoted in this work fill me with such hope.
Some commentators seem to have gone as far as saying that even calling
Amida's name just once may be enough: "All people, without discrimi-*

nation between old and young, male and female, who recite nembutsu ten times, or just once, will be, with certainty, embraced by the grace of the essential vow of Amida Buddha who never abandons anyone" (Hōnen). *Seemingly too easy and too good to be true, and I am certainly embarrassed by such a hope. But any notion of rigour that I previously held onto as a serious spiritual seeker is quickly evaporating into the dark haze of spiritual ineptitude. Death worries me immensely as I have squandered, it seems, every opportunity afforded me to be saved.*

The more I get to know you over the years, the more convinced I am that you are an exceptional candidate for the Primal Vow. The person who is stumbling in a 'dark haze of spiritual ineptitude' is exactly who Amida is reaching out to. He has vowed to do this precisely because of the spiritual ailments that have led you to this impasse. In any case, your very recognition of this is a clear indication that Amida is already working within you—it is none other than the onset of the wisdom that helps you to see things as they are. But this insight, which enables you to become mindful of your disturbing passions is, at the same time, always accompanied by the awareness that we are taken into and protected by this Vow 'that grasps never to abandon'.

As for the efficacy of a single recitation—yes, it is true that this is quite adequate provided it is motivated by a genuine desire for birth in the Pure Land (a desire that can only have its genesis in Amida's calling). In reality, though, nobody ever really invokes the Name only once as the dawning of faith leads to its spontaneous arising throughout one's life (even if infrequently—the actual number is irrelevant). The first faith-based utterance of the nembutsu is what is critical as it indicates the 'breaking-through' of Amida's light for the first time, and that is why Hōnen says that it is perfectly sufficient—subsequent recitations then become expressions of both gratitude and the ongoing presence of Amida's spiritual influence. So, no, you have not 'squandered every opportunity' to be saved and neither should you feel 'embarrassed' by the hope offered by this Dharma. If anything, it should be a cause for joy and celebration. For people like us, there really is no other way.

Q: My reading has, once again, highlighted for me the issue of attaining shinjin and the role of recitative nembutsu. We have come to hear the

Name and, in turn, we say it, having therefore encountered Amida's Vow in some form, even if it is not fully realised as shinjin. So where does that leave the great majority who will never attain shinjin? Birth in the Shin tradition is equated to Nirvāna itself, but doesn't the tradition speak of various levels of birth in the Pure Land?

Hearing the Name and responding to this call through the nembutsu is—precisely—what shinjin is. The invocation that follows 'hearing' or *monpo* is what defines the awakening of faith in each person. And, yes, indeed there are various levels of birth and all of them entail salvation. The Pure Land, broadly considered, is more than just Nirvāna and, seeing as it transcends samsāra, there is no suffering to be found there. Even those who say the Name with some doubt have established a connection with Amida Buddha and so they are no longer subject to further transmigration. All states in the Pure Land are happy ones, from which full enlightenment is much more easily attained. Shinjin is distinctive in that it provides a direct means of realising Nirvāna, which is the ultimate goal of Buddhist endeavour. However, faithful adherents of the Pure Land teaching who never attain shinjin in this life are still saved nevertheless. But I think it is a mistake to assume that shinjin is some kind of rarefied state that eludes most people, like *satori* in Zen. It is true that shinjin is not common but that is not necessarily because its requirements lie beyond the reach of ordinary people. The history of this tradition is there to demonstrate otherwise. In summary, not everyone who is saved in the Pure Land has necessarily attained Nirvāna and one does not have to have realised shinjin in order to be born in Amida's realm of happiness.

[margin note: what if no shinjin ? → we are still saved !]

Q: You have previously stated the following: 'To simply recite the nembutsu with no other motive than to attain blissful entry into Nirvāna for oneself is doomed to failure because the incentive then appears to be solely one of self-gain uninformed by either gratitude to the Buddha or compassion for one's suffering fellow beings'. While I understand the ugliness of invoking the Name in such a way, will it not be the attitude the majority have in this last Dharma-ending age of Mappō? Even though shinjin may be impossible for such a person, will not invoking the name still bring with it a salvific transition? Though the majority of us will end up in the borderlands, this is surely better than to continue wandering in the rounds of samsāra.

I certainly understand your concern here. What is 'doomed to failure' in the passage you cite is the attainment of enlightenment, not 'salvation'. It is important to keep this distinction in mind. People who do not attain shinjin in this life, even though they are devoted to the nembutsu (albeit imperfectly), are no longer subject to the round of saṃsāra but go, as you say, to the borderland or the Womb Palace which—unquestionably—is not a place of suffering. In time, and through greater maturation in a more spiritually favourable realm, our passage to the true Pure Land is assured. Just because we do not realise Nirvāna at the time of death, does not mean that we are abandoned—Amida's acceptance is always there. All nembutsu devotees go to happier destinations—it is just that their journey may not yet be complete.

Q: I suppose what I am asking is that if Amida's light and life are unhindered, their efficacy should remain unaffected by anything we do on our side. Though our initial intent may not be consonant with the Primal Vow, surely the continued invocation will slowly bring us into accord with it until such time that it becomes natural or effortless, and we are no longer the one invoking. At this stage, whatever motive we had to begin with would have dissolved into gratitude.

This is largely correct. However, you suggest that the efficacy of Amida's light 'should remain unaffected by anything we do on our side'. This is true only to the extent that we have already begun to engage with the teaching and made ourselves open and responsive to the Buddha's light. Although shinjin is 'unearned', so to speak, it still must be wholeheartedly accepted by us, otherwise it cannot bring about its transformative work.

Q: If self-powered invocation is, in reality, Other-power invocation, whose true depth cannot have been known by us initially due to our karma obscuring its inconceivable power, the fact that we have invoked the Name, even if it be once, suggests that our karma has ripened sufficiently for the Call to be heard. Even if we say Amida's name just once, without depth, without commitment and without awakening the aspiration for enlightenment and the desire to save all beings, will we already be saved from samsāra after death, even if it be in the borderlands? The question is important because the knowledge that we are already saved, no matter how shallow our commitment is, seems to me an important precursor to 'gratitudinal' nembutsu.

Again, I quite agree although I do not believe that any and every invocation of the nembutsu is spiritually efficacious. Merely saying the Name, in and of itself, is not enough. One could say it, for example, out of idle curiosity or even mockery. Neither do I feel that anyone who genuinely believes that they 'are already saved' can be said to have shallow faith—such a belief already constitutes a significant realisation! The only commitment that is required is recitation of the Name coupled with a desire to be born in the Pure Land. In fact, you could say that this very desire is the catalyst for the recitation with the desire itself being the working of Amida. The arising of faith is a mystery and I would be loath to make judgements on whose faith is deep or shallow or even 'sufficient'. However, some level of aspiration is needed otherwise we cannot be said to have 'heard' the call of the Buddha at all. This is what establishes the karmic connection that initiates our journey back to the Pure Land. Our invocation is the response to the Buddha's summons to return home. The fact that we sincerely desire this is a sign that we accept Amida's wish to liberate us and thus we surrender to him accordingly (and leave our posthumous destinies to his care). This is already a profound shift in our consciousness and could hardly be described as 'without depth, without commitment and without awakening'.

Q: Another question I have concerns your essay 'Reflections on Gensō-Ekō'. While our return to this world is a return as Amida, or as an agent of the Primal Vow, it does however make the following statement in the Tannishō somewhat hard to understand: 'If, however, simply abandoning self-power, we quickly attain enlightenment in the Pure Land, we will be able to save first, by means of transcendent powers, those with whom we have close karmic relations, whatever karmic suffering they may have sunk to in the six realms through the four modes of birth'. If our individuality is dissolved in the Land of Bliss, and our return is Amida's return, how are we to make sense of 'save . . . first those with whom we have close karmic relations'? This would imply that some residue of our karmic past still remains in the Land of Bliss.

This is an excellent observation. Indeed, I have struggled with this question for many years. My essay on *gensō-ekō* was simply an honest attempt at reconciling Shinran's teaching with the (in my view) all-important doctrine of *anattā*. I have never been quite satisfied with how this question has been resolved by some teachers so I decided to go out on a limb and present another perspective on the matter. There are certainly passages in Shinran where he suggests that the attainment of Nirvāna is a state transcending mere individual personality rather than personality as such. Amida represents the perfection and consummation of personality (indeed Nāgārjuna refers to him as the 'Pure Person') and I imagine that people of shinjin assume that same 'personality' as well when they attain perfect enlightenment.

Now, of course, a literal reading of what Shinran says above suggests that we continue to maintain a personal interest in our loved ones from beyond the grave. This has given immense hope and comfort to millions of people so far be it for me to suggest that it is not true! But perhaps it is true in a higher sense than that suggested by that passage in the *Tannishō*. What I mean is that the force that saves all beings (including our loved ones) is one and the same, namely the power of Amida's Primal Vow; not something that is scattered or divided among countless distinct bodhisattvas. Those who enter Nirvāna become part of this great salvific current which reaches out to all sentient beings without discrimination. At this level of realisation, the spiritual plight of particular individuals in this world becomes the concern of all bodhisattvas who act in unison or, more precisely, becomes the object of the 'bodhisattvic' force inherent in Suchness. The spiritual care of those with whom we have 'close karmic relations' is still there but it's not just 'us' (as an individual) who carries this out from the Pure Land but becomes the responsibility of nirvanic reality itself with which we have completely identified ourselves. Here, we are on the cusp of what is expressible and perhaps there is not much more to be said but I do feel that Shinran's position on *gensō-ekō* is certainly true, even if not in a strictly literal sense.

By way of conclusion, the most important thing to remember is that Amida's compassion is unfathomable. Even if someone, who had passed away, knew nothing about Buddhism, or had no religious outlook, they may certainly be reborn in any number of the Buddhist heavens based on their good karma in this life. Now, these heavens are purportedly extremely pleasant but they are still in samsāra and so transitory (though of much greater duration than human life). The Buddha is present in all realms (including the hells which are also ephemeral) so no one is ever without hope as the Buddha is constantly working to bring all beings to the Land of Light.

Q: *The role of Dharmākara has always been problematic to me in the sense of the 'greater coming from the lesser'. I understand Dharmākara being a manifestation of the Trikāya but the vocational journey of Dharmākara through aeons of perfect practice to establish the fulfillment of the Vows, still remains an issue in that the finite cannot give rise to the infinite. Now, the whole issue of mythology and symbolism excludes a too literal understanding of Dharmākara, but the idea of invoking the highest reality also excludes the possibility that the reality being invoked could have, at any stage, been less than absolute. Does the Trikāya solve this? Well, it creates a kind of chicken and egg problem in my mind. The vows exist because of Dharmākara's pledges as a bodhisattva. However, if Amida Buddha is an expression of the Dharma-Body, his infinite virtues must have pre-existed the bodhisattva, as must have the vow to save all beings. So, in a sense, when we invoke Amida, we invoke the absolute personal expression of the Dharma-Body in its intrinsic nature as saving compassion.*

The Dharmākara narrative continues to cause difficulties for many Westerners especially. I used to be perplexed by the same questions as you—my concern was how could that which Shinran considered to be, effectively, infinite and eternal (Amida) have an original in space and time (the actions of Dharmākara in history)? I finally came to the view that the practice of the bodhisattva did not take place in any kind of history as we understand it. I do not see it as a one-off 'event' but rather as an expression of the fundamental compassion at the heart of ultimate reality. It is not as if this will to save sentient beings did not exist prior to Dharmākara's vows so, in that sense, they are integral to this reality. One could say that the sūtra depicts eternal verities in the guise of 'cause-and-effect' in order to humanise this compassion and make it accessible to us. In the end, the very power said to have been generated by Dharmākara through his aeons of practice must be the same power that has always been inherent in Suchness or the Dharma-Body. If so, one can only conclude that the story represents spiritual fact, to be sure, but not historical fact (in terms of ordinary samsaric time); in other words, a myth must be, as I recall reading somewhere, a 'horizontal' narrative about a 'vertical' reality. This is the only way I can reconcile myself to the sūtra narrative while also respecting those views, particularly in Japan, that consider Dharmākara to have been a real person in the distant historical past, however that is envisaged.

Q: I have just read the following passage from the Larger Sūtra where the Buddha says to Ananda, "As soon as the Bhiksu Dharmākara spoke those verses, the entire earth shook in six ways and a rain of wonderful flowers fell from heaven, scattering everywhere. Spontaneous music was heard and a voice in the sky said, 'Surely you will attain the highest, perfect Enlightenment'". What is the traditional interpretation of the 'voice in the sky'? All these manifestations seem to be a transcendent affirmation of Dharmākara's vows and perhaps even proof of their nirvanic origin. I have read it before but, this time, it struck me as being of great significance.

The confirmation from the 'voice in the sky' is indeed quite significant. I recall seeing this in other sūtras as well (where the future success of a bodhisattva's vows is prophesied) but I think it has greater import in the *Larger Sūtra* in light of what is at stake. The voice, clearly, cannot be that of Dharmākara's master, the Buddha Lokeshvararaja, because he would have been physically present to the bodhisattva before whom the vows were made. In a sense, it denotes the 'endorsement' of nirvanic reality itself from which Dharmākara has emerged. As you point out, 'sky' of course refers to the transcendent and thus is an affirmation from beyond this world which, in turn, guarantees the efficacy of the vows.

Q: I am trying to reconcile two statements from D. T. Suzuki:

> *"The pronouncing of the Name is possible only when the devotee's own 'inner Amida', so to speak, is awakened from the darkness of ignorance. When the latter event does not take place, the pronouncing of the Name is mere shadow with nothing really backing it; there is no correspondence between reality and expression, between content and form, between heart and lips."*

If there was no correspondence between reality and expression when repeating the name without a requisite awakening of our 'inner Amida', then the following quote makes little sense. The fact that the named and the name do indeed have a correspondence makes the 'process of rearrangement in the consciousness of the practiser' possible:

> *'The repeated pronouncing of Amida's Name, however mechanical and contentless in the beginning, gradually sets up a process of rearrangement in the consciousness of the practiser who becomes thus unwittingly aware of the presence of Amida in his own inner being. When this moment is realised, he utters for the first time—*

from the depths of his soul—the Name of Amida as the power lift-ing him from the burden of karma. . . . The psychological tone of consciousness created by continuous recitation will one day, when time matures, prepare the way for the devotee to the awakening of faith in Amida'.

You have always made it clear that the nembutsu is not 'magical' or mantric in nature; but if it is the form chosen by Amida to make himself available to all in order to fulfill his Vow to save everyone—a Vow whose completion and perfection has already been guaranteed—the nembutsu cannot therefore be in vain, no matter how shallow the invocation is, for it participates, at least formally, in the identity between the Name and that which is Named.

I think Suzuki is tackling the issue from different but complementary angles. There are also some unspoken assumptions in his statements. Every recitation of the Name, however shallow, is 'backed up', so to speak, by the presence of Amida Buddha. Merely mouthing the words—by a mocking sceptic for example—is not likely to effect a 'rearrangement in their consciousness'. The tradition is very clear in saying that the nembutsu is a response to 'hearing the Name' (i.e., conceiving joy in awakening to Amida's Vow and its full significance). If someone knows next to nothing about the Dharma or the Pure Land way but simply says *Namo Amida Butsu* (as if to prove that it is a meaningless utterance), then there is nothing in the sound of that phrase to effect some kind of miraculous transformation in the spiritual awareness of that person, contrary to their will. There has to be a sense in which one is actually seeking truth or emancipation and thus open to Amida's grace.

Therefore, as I have mentioned before, the nembutsu is an embodiment of the awakening of faith. In other words, it is the 'form' this faith takes in the individual's life. When Suzuki says 'however mechanical and contentless in the beginning . . .', he does not, in my view, suggest that there is no foundation of faith even here (however attenuated)—just that one's nembutsu may initially be tentative and unsure. People in this situation (and this certainly describes me in my early days) feel the need to say the Name often, even to the point of forcing themselves, but this reflects a less developed 'self–power' attitude in the practiser who believes that intense recitation will somehow provoke the realisation of shinjin or the experience of

Amida's embrace. Now, of course, Amida's working is behind these efforts as well and this phase is what helps in the 'rearrangement of consciousness' that Suzuki refers to. Perhaps he could have expressed himself in a more nuanced way but I think what he means is that this 'rearrangement' leads to a transformation whereby the Name starts to arise more spontaneously as one's shinjin deepens. It may be helpful to consider the awakening of faith as a spectrum, ranging from a nascent stage to a more mature consummation.

My view is that the identity of the Name and the Named only becomes a reality when the former is heard and invoked with faith, i.e., when the nembutsu comes from the Buddha (which also presupposes propitious karmic conditions because, clearly, not everyone is spiritually liberated in this life). The fact that Amida's vow guarantees to save all does not mean that it imposes no requirements. At a minimum, it demands some kind of response and acceptance of the Vow from the devotee. Otherwise, the salvific seed cannot be sown or take root. We must 'admit' the Buddha into our hearts so that his working can take effect.

I certainly understand your desire to 'lower the bar' of salvation as much as possible. However, more people are 'saved' (i.e., reach the non–retrogressive stage) than attain Nirvāna immediately after death and shinjin is certainly not a prerequisite for salvation in the broad sense; which means that even those who recite the Name faithfully, albeit with some doubt, anxiety or lack of steadfastness, will all be freed from the sufferings of samsāra.

Q: I came across a Japanese Shinshū scholar who states that it was the Dharma-Body itself that incarnated as Dharmākara. The identity of the Dharma-Body and Amida is thereby made explicit, and I remember you describing Amida as the 'personal' face of the Dharma-Body. Amida is not just another Buddha and, even though all Buddhas are, in essence, of the Dharma-Body, and invoking or worshipping them is, in effect, referencing the Absolute, Amida is the Supreme Buddha in Whom all other Buddhas may be subsumed.

Regarding your remarks about Dharmākara, Shinran himself actually said 'Manifesting a form from this (formless) treasure-ocean of Suchness, calling himself Dharmākara Bodhisattva, and making the unhindered Vows as the causes, he became Amida Buddha'. In that sense, you are quite right—Amida is more than 'just another Buddha' but a manifestation of the wisdom and compassion inherent in ultimate reality itself.

Q: I remember Shinran saying something about the borderlands being a world without pain, even though they would not be content or happy there. Is that correct?

The Jōdo Shinshū perspective is not inclined to consider the borderlands as places of suffering seeing as they do not form part of samsāra—they are clearly a dimension or 'extension' of the Pure Land itself. Shinran says that one does not suffer there, except insofar as one is deprived of the immediate presence of Amida Buddha but one is not aware of this at first. This realm, also known as the 'Womb Palace', is essentially a place of benign expiation (unlike the hells) so no pain is experienced by its denizens. They are only there because they harbour residual doubts about the efficacy of the Buddha's Vow, not because they have slandered the Dharma or anything like that. Essentially, they are those who have practised according to the 19th and 20th Vows (rare enough as that is!) so their sojourn there is a form of mild correction (and not unpleasant in any way) until such time as they realise the truth of the 18th Vow which enables them to finally abandon all reservations and surrender completely to Amida, thus attaining perfect Nirvāna.

(d) *Exchanges with a correspondent*

Comment: Provisional truth is used to lead to a greater truth and I am not sure that a sensuous understanding of higher states and realms is completely incompatible with a more metaphysical understanding. Besides, the descriptions are such that everything in the Pure Land provokes an apprehension of the Dharma:

> "*When a gentle breeze wafts through its branches and leaves, innumerable exquisite Dharma sounds arise, which spread far and wide, pervading all the other buddha lands in the ten directions. Those who hear the sounds attain penetrating insight into dharmas and dwell in the stage of non-retrogression*" (*Larger Sūtra of Immeasurable Life*).

Even the most literal understanding of the sūtras will find its appeal beyond an ordinary understanding according to the senses, but will draw from an imaginal conception deeply infused with a sense of something greater. This is precisely the power of the sūtras, and why post-modern approaches to such texts completely miss the mark. Providing it does not warp into something delusional and self-satisfying, then there is no issue. I read the Pure Land sūtras in quite a literal way but, as with the extract above, it is understood that the Dharma pervades every aspect of that experience.

Yes indeed—I completely agree. I was only surmising that Rennyo would have come across followers, in his time, who may have been drawn to the prospect of continuing to enjoy (more intensely in the next life) the pleasures they enjoyed in this world without fully apprehending the pervading nature of the Dharma behind the sūtra descriptions. I daresay many in his congregation would not have had a deep acquaintance with Buddhist doctrine and might easily have formed an unbalanced view regarding this question (thus impairing their understanding of shinjin). Even so, it may well be sufficient to aspire for the Pure Land (however conceived) and allow the 'saving means' of Amida Buddha to take care of the rest.

Comment: Agreed but I have the recurring intuition that encountering the Dharma in itself ensures the efficacy of the nembutsu; that even though karma is inscrutable, ultimately nothing is 'accidental'. This is complicated by the bodhisattva ideal, implicit in Amida's Vows, to use every skilful means to lead beings to Enlightenment. So if we encounter the nembutsu, my intuition is that it cannot be fortuitous and that there has been some intent behind this encounter, even if this is rendered through karmic forces.

The efficacy of the nembutsu is tied up with the awakening of faith so, in a sense, encountering the Dharma (which is certainly not accidental) leads to both at the same time. I think you are correct in saying that the intent of the Vow is 'rendered through karmic forces' but, in this case, these forces are the result of the Vow's pure merit which seeks to overcome our own unfavourable karma. In his book *The Way of Nembutsu-Faith* (note that *nembutsu* and *faith* are treated as one and the same here), Dr Inagaki says: "Faith without nembutsu is impossible and nembutsu without faith is fruitless. . . . We do not say the nembutsu because we believe that it is the cause of our salvation—we say it with no reason whatever on our part. On the one hand, we are too ignorant to discern between true and false, right and wrong. On the other hand, in our experience of shinjin, the presence of Amida Buddha is beyond any doubt. . . . Since the nembutsu is Amida's Mind and Body, it does not belong to me. However many times we may recite it, it does not become ours but remains his . . . Shinjin and nembutsu are thus Amida's self-expression through our hearts and mouths."

Comment: I understand but Amida is, necessarily, coercing us because the bodhisattva ideal requires him to do so. A bodhisattva makes vows to save beings by any and every skilful means (i.e., coercion or manipulation at the very least). Amida has the ultimate skillful means—the call to the Pure Land and the transference of merit to exhaust karmic debt.

True, but Amida aims to influence our will, not force it. Of course, if someone turns their back on the Vow or rejects the Buddha's invitation (or, as is more likely in our times, dismisses the reality of such things altogether), the Buddha does not give up on them but continues to employ all manner of upāya to win them over. If you make choices based on such a rejection, there will be karmic consequences for you—Amida cannot intervene in that sense (because even this rejection itself has karmic antecedents)—and thus the Buddha's salvific work must, necessarily, take longer.

Comment: So this is from Other-Power, which means that we are already under Amida's influence. Therefore, we are responding to the call with the nembutsu and invocation implies faith of sorts in that being invoked. Is this therefore the first nascent form of shinjin, even though we are not aware of Other-Power in our nembutsu?

Yes, Amida's influence is always present—it is just that our receptivity to it is initially wanting. When we eventually encounter that influence for the first time as the Buddha's call, we respond with the nembutsu but one that implies, as you say, 'faith of sorts in that being invoked'. This is indeed the 'first nascent form of shinjin' (because Amida's working has already started to take effect even though we may not have fully assimilated all its implications). As shinjin starts to settle and deepen, we begin to realise the Other-Power dimension in our nembutsu invocation.

Comment: But even Shinran did not know whether the nembutsu would lead him to hell or not! Perhaps I am being too 'calculating' in trying to understand this. Shinran may have expressed his doubt outwardly but as a rejection of his calculating self. A 'natural' Amida-given confidence (shinjin) leaves no room for self-confidence.

I do not believe that Shinran's remarks regarding 'whether the *nembutsu* would lead him to hell or not' are evidence of any real uncertainty on his part. They were aimed at a particular audience—the authorities of traditional Buddhism who were condemning him as a heretic—as well as being an affirmation of his devotion to Hōnen. It is indeed true that he urged people to avoid making all-too-human calculations regarding our posthumous destiny because, as you rightly point out, an 'Amida-given confidence' regarding our birth in the Pure Land effectively neutralises any calculation (*hakarai*) on our part.

Comment: How are we to understand this remark from a Pure Land master?:

> *"Our hands are now empty: we know not if we have acquired faith or not. Amida's work is to save us assuredly; and our work is to fall into hell."*

Paradoxically, this is a remark from someone who has already realised shinjin! It is not, despite appearances, an expression of genuine doubt. Anybody who is able to say: '. . . but we are satisfied and eternal peace abides in our minds' (which is the very next line in that passage) is surely someone whose faith is deeply settled. So I think the important insight here is that our ego is unable to make any kind of judgement regarding such matters. The awareness of shinjin comes from Amida but we, nevertheless, experience it as individuals even though it does not have its source in us as ordinary *bombu*.

(e) *Responses to various correspondents*

In the end, what you must understand is that the Buddha's compassion will never abandon you, especially since you feel the ardent need for it and are so hungry for its blessings. The generosity and compassion at the heart of existence never accepts 'spiritual scoundrels' grudgingly—indeed, the recognition of our indigence is the very realisation that makes this compassion known to us for the first time. If the nembutsu is coming to you unprompted, then just take it in your stride and see where it leads you. There is no point in adding to your stresses by doing violence to your natural inclinations. No encounter with Amida Buddha is wasted; it will always be a wonderful opportunity for inner growth and succour, regardless of your other circumstances. In this way, it can only serve to enrich your spiritual journey, wherever it may take you.

*   *   *

You say that 'it makes me depressed to see saṃsāra as a sea of sorrow and despair' but that is exactly what saṃsāra is! Look around and you will receive abundant confirmation of this fact throughout the world and in everyone's lives. This is why the Buddha's teaching is so confronting for people—but that does not make it any less true. But wouldn't it be even more depressing if there was no exit from such a rueful state of affairs? This is the joyous aspect of the Buddha's teaching; namely, that there can be a permanent end to suffering through one's complete surrender to Amida Buddha. The spiritual life is a paradox. We feel the suffering in the world most deeply but, at the same time, we rejoice in knowing that this life is but a passing shadow on our journey to the Land of Infinite Light. It does not make the shadow go away, of course, but it enables us to overcome it spiritually. We can feel the presence of this light even now and this confirms both the truth of the Buddha's teaching as well as providing us with the strength to endure saṃsāra (where we can help others to discover the same truth). In the end, the solace we receive is in coming to see that Amida is unending life and that our true self, our Buddha-nature, will be restored to the realm of peace and happiness.

*   *   *

When I mentioned that 'I don't worry about shinjin', it is not because I believe that I do not have it or am unsure about it. I simply do not engage in this question as an act of *hakarai*. After a long period of 'hearing' and nembutsu, there is a gradual shift in one's consciousness

171

where the presence of Amida feels certain and immediate—but it is not entirely up to us as to when this happens. So, of course, shinjin is very important but, as it is something that emerges when the karmic conditions are ripe, there is no need for us to be overly concerned about it. It still must be tested and refined as we travel on the path, but this just means that our shinjin is never fixed or frozen in time. The fact that our faith can deepen does not mean that our birth is uncertain—only that there is endless room for a more penetrating awareness commensurate with the boundless nature of Amida's Light.

* * *

It is important to distinguish Other-Power from self-effort. There is a danger of becoming completely passive with respect to one's everyday life because one thinks the Buddha is taking care of everything. I think this can cause problems in that a completely deterministic perspective on our behaviour is psychologically unhealthy. I do believe we make free choices in life—Amida can certainly illuminate such choices but I do not believe that he causes them (like a puppet master). Now, depending on the depth of your shinjin, chances are that Amida's influence will often be irresistible and therefore one's actions take a natural course. But things are not always that clear—we often make bad decisions in life and we cannot say, surely, that Amida is behind every poor choice that is made. Often our minds are just too dark and confused with respect to secular matters even if our spiritual life feels sheltered by the Buddha.

In this sense, I accept the remark that the Tathagata assumes 'the burden of my every responsibility'. Note that it still remains my responsibility—it is just that Amida is there for me regardless of the mistakes and bad judgements I make because they will ultimately have no karmic consequences for me beyond the present life.

I also agree with Kiyozawa's view that 'if even life and death are no longer of concern, then surely there is no need to worry about things of lesser importance'. Yes, Amida's wisdom allows us to put things in proper perspective in light of our 'commitment to the Infinite'. However, even this outlook respects the reality of human free will.

And, yes, we are powerless over so many things in life but that does not, of course, make us karmic robots! Assuredly, we are 'within the hands of a power beyond self' and this entrusting can enrich our lives immeasurably without determining every facet of it.

Finally, it is certainly true that Amida has 'paid our karmic debts' and this is a huge burden lifted from us. So, in a sense, we must 'let this world go as it does' with respect to what we cannot change. But, in the end, we are still encouraged to be 'skillful' with our lives and make decisions that conform to the Dharma.

*　*　*

I do not consciously follow the precepts or any sundry practices for the simple reason that I am incapable of doing so. I also do not think that pursuing such practices makes any difference to my salvation. I hope that is clear enough. However, as you say, a person of shinjin can either spontaneously follow some of the precepts or feel a deep impulse to do so, even if the result is imperfect. This, of course, is very different from wanting to follow them because one has a particular spiritual objective in mind. Nevertheless, I do acknowledge that if I was capable of following some of the Buddha's injunctions more faithfully, my life may very well run more smoothly. But this is what it means to be a *bombu* afflicted with *bonnō*. On a daily basis, I see what I ought to do but often fail to do it, through either weakness or perversity of will. Had I done it, though, the consequences to my life would be very different.

Therefore, I do try to improve my behaviour—not for the sake of 'salvation'—but as a courtesy to other human beings. I hate it when I am cruel, rude or selfish even though I know Amida accepts this about me, but I am still keen to work on myself, to the extent possible, because it helps to make life less painful for myself and others. Some Shin Buddhists think that, because they are simple *bombu*, they have no obligation to correct bad behaviour as they feel that, to do so, is somehow in vain. This simply isn't true—I refer you to Shinran's famous letter on the subject in the *Mattōshō*. It is a facile way of avoiding personal responsibility for one's actions to claim that one is just stupid or ignorant and thus incapable of acting any differently. Shinran makes it clear that the arising of shinjin does lead to a certain modification in our behaviour, even though we can never attain perfection. So there this is no excuse for indifference or laziness where this can, legitimately, be avoided.

The other aspect of 'effort' is in relation to spiritual practice. People think that because shinjin is 'given' by Amida, it somehow falls out of the sky. We forget that much preparation often goes into becoming receptive to the Buddha's influence. I struggled with Shinran's writings for a very long time before things started to become a little clearer. One doesn't just sit on a couch for twenty years watching television all day hoping that something magical will happen. The path—even though it is based on 'Other Power'—calls for engagement. This is not effort with a view to 'earning' spiritual freedom but in order to enable us to 'hear the Light' more deeply. If not for this, why doesn't everyone already have shinjin? Certainly, there are karmic considerations in the awakening of faith but it also involves work on our part. This may take either the form of spending years of *jiriki* practice in another tradition and realising its futility or intense study of the Pure Land sūtras with a view to discerning the profundities of Amida's Vow. Do not forget that Shinran himself went through the 19th and 20th Vows before he turned to the 18th—this involved, you can be sure, much struggle and effort over many years. Some would say that Shinran went through all this travail so that we need not have to. This is true but I have found it very rare for someone to have directly entered the path of the 18th Vow without a preceding period of spiritual hardship.

Yes, Shin is the 'easy' path because our emancipation from samsāra is assured by Amida Buddha but only if our faith has been awakened. And what does Shinran say about this? "Of all things difficult, it is the most difficult." He also says that "the way to the Pure Land is easy but very few go there". Therefore, for me at least, there is volitional effort insofar as I strive to understand Shinran as deeply as possible; and this I do because of my veneration for his teachings. Even if my intellectual grasp of, say, the *Kyōgyōshinshō* is extremely shallow and I give up, I am still embraced by the Buddha because of my faith. However, correct faith does not emerge in a vacuum—it requires an accurate 'hearing' of the Dharma and deep reflection on its significance, even if this entails only grasping the basic meaning of *Namo Amida Butsu* (as many illiterate peasants in Shinran's time could only do).

As to your final point, I understand what you are saying. It is quite true, in my experience, that the reality of shinjin not only gives me assurance of finally attaining Nirvāna but, even in this life, it gives me the wisdom of the Buddha with which I am able to more successfully navigate the treacherous waters of samsāra in my everyday affairs. It allows me to be less self-centred and to see beauty and wonder where previously I did not. It definitely enriches my mundane existence and, indeed, helps me to see the 'oneness' of things (even though duality is never entirely eliminated for an unenlightened *bombu*). Perhaps what people mean when they speak about relying on themselves in secular matters is that they do not engage in petitionary prayer. For example, while you may ask Amida to bestow his wisdom and compassion on you, you would not normally ask for health, love, money, professional success or some other worldly benefit. Such boons are just as much determined by karmic considerations as they are by the quality of our personal judgements.

Jōdo Shinshū is keen to contrast itself to groups such as Sōka Gakkai where religion is largely used for gaining wealth and temporal advantages; in doing so, however, it sometimes goes too far and seems to reject the 'this-worldly' benefits of shinjin (of which Shinran reminds us when he talks about the 'ten benefits' of faith in this life). So, yes, realising our oneness with Amida (but note this is never separate from our awareness of 'non-oneness' as well) is absolutely fundamental but, spiritually speaking, this is the only benefit that matters. The 'overall conditioning of all the myriad things' can also lead to people of shinjin leading terrible lives full of pain, suffering and misery (notwithstanding their faith) so the point is that having become awakened to our fundamental unity with the Buddha does not mean that we necessarily accrue any mundane blessings in this world.

* * *

I accept, of course, the insights of our Pure Land masters regarding the true nature of samsara. Indeed, it is the acute dismay at our existential plight that heightens our aspiration for the Land of Bliss. This darkness that we often sense about the world (which can often be heightened in people of faith) manifests itself differently in everyday life according to the conditions of one's karma. For some people, it still allows them to lead a positive and meaningful life; for others, it can lead to self-destruction and cause great suffering to others.

We all manifest our 'shadow' aspect in varied ways but I am not convinced that negative responses are always inevitable. I believe our human behaviours can be assisted and while not being an advocate of every form of psychological therapy (far from it), I have seen direct evidence that it can be helpful (both for spiritual and non-spiritual types). We all have a worldly side and, of course, secular solutions can work for people. It would be a shame to so easily dismiss potentially helpful options which one may not have tried. Obviously, this kind of treatment does not make the darkness go away (it is not meant to) but it can help us to better integrate it into our lives so that any harm to our psyche is minimised. This is not about diverting us from the truth of suffering but containing its worst manifestations for ourselves and others.

Yes, deeper surrender to Amida is, naturally, a desirable thing but it does not always lead to greater compassion or loving kindness. Selfishness will always inform who we are as ordinary mortals and there is no accounting for what lurks beneath the surface of our conventional self. As Shinran says, we are all capable of becoming murderers should the karmic causes present themselves—a life of shinjin offers no guarantee of saintly behaviour. Nevertheless, a 'good friend in the dharma' (*zenjishiki*), while deeply flawed in many ways like the rest of us, can still serve as an effective spiritual teacher.

* * *

Do not be overly concerned about feeling insufficient gratitude. It is one possibility among others for manifesting our shinjin and you most certainly should not see it as a sign that you are lacking true faith. Shinran himself often experienced this himself and spoke about it most poignantly. Awakening to Amida's true and real mind—this is all that matters. How we individually respond to this awakening is a matter of karma and personal disposition; it is not something that is subject to strict criteria or rules.

* * *

As you say, Shinran went through the practice of the Three Vows himself before settling into the path of shinjin so, if that was good enough for him, far be it for us to think we are above it! While I understand the concerns of the scholar you mentioned, ordinary people do need something concrete and reciting the Name is a very effective way of keeping us grounded in an accessible practice. Indeed, Shinran does say that reciting the Name with aspiration—

even if one's faith is not entirely settled—can lead to the arising of shinjin, naturally and spontaneously of itself. Some scholars try to dismiss this by suggesting that this was an earlier teaching of Shinran's which he subsequently never mentioned again but I do not believe this is true. It speaks to a very real condition that faces all beginners and which I think Shinran addresses in a most compassionate manner. Of course, Hōnen's notion 'that you can recite the nembutsu while walking, standing, sitting or lying down' is also applicable to Shinran who never aimed to restrict its recitation in everyday circumstances.

* * *

Yes, *upāya* is often relegated, by some, to the status of a convenient fiction but, as you point out, it really is the 'dynamic' aspect of the truth. In fact, it is the only way that truth can reach us at all in our world of forms. An upāya, therefore, is not a human contrivance but the compassionate approach towards sentient beings by the highest reality. If not for this, spiritual truth would remain inconceivable and beyond our ken.

* * *

Your question regarding the so-called Amida 'myth' is a very good one as it is an issue that clearly exercises many people approaching Shin Buddhism for the first time. In Japan, it is not uncommon to encounter the view that Dharmākara was a real bodhisattva who walked this earth and undertook the practices as described in the *Larger Sūtra*. As you say, this gives people a real sense of foundation behind the salvific activity of Amida Buddha. In fact, I have often met old Shin folk in Kyoto whose eyes well up with tears as they reflect on the sacrifices made by this bodhisattva on behalf of ordinary people. I am always deeply impressed when I encounter this but I never see it among Western Shin followers! Americans and Europeans, on the whole, simply see the sūtra events as stories concocted by Shakyamuni (or subsequent sages) as a way of helping people to understand the compassionate nature of Amida Buddha. Like many people, I struggled with this question for many years and am now thinking that, perhaps, the answer lies somewhere in the middle.

Firstly, I do not think that Dharmākara was a historical figure in our time—the sūtra clearly does not require us to believe that, especially when you consider the inconceivable cosmic timescales of which it speaks. Otherwise, one faces absurd statements like one I heard from a 'literalist' who claimed that Dharmākara must have been around during the time of the dinosaurs! I think the truth of the matter is a little more nuanced than that. We must remember that the sūtra writers, like many other Indian thinkers of the time, were not really interested in documenting historical events (such as we find narrated in the Gospels for example). They were primarily concerned with spiritual truth and were inspired to use the full resources of their powerful imaginations to convey this as vividly and powerfully as they could. Now, it may well be that the sūtra story is describing events in another realm or spiritual universe that is unknown to us— in fact, a number of thoughtful Western Shin Buddhists believe exactly that. This exempts them from any obligation to accept these events as having taken place on this earth but still allows them to view the story as true in a universal sense.

However, things become a little more complicated when we consider Shinran's take on the matter. Philosophically, he was somewhat more sophisticated than his teacher, Hōnen, and keen to ground the Pure Land teachings in the metaphysical roots of the Mahāyāna. For example, Shinran did not consider the Pure Land as just a place where you continue your Buddhist practice in a more spiritually favourable environment surrounded by jewelled trees, light-emitting lotuses, flowers raining from the sky and other delights. He essentially considered it, in its real aspect, as the equivalent of Nirvāna (thus, his reference to it as the 'True' Pure Land). As you would appreciate, Nirvāna is a boundless reality—it does not have an origin in time or space so it cannot have simply been created through the meritorious actions of a bodhisattva or anything like that. Similarly, Shinran tends towards a view of Amida Buddha as absolute, limitless and without measure; therefore, also as a reality without origin. Accordingly, the 'foundation' for both Amida and the Pure Land is none other than the Dharma-Body, Suchness or Nirvāna itself.

Nevertheless, Shinran did not just dismiss the 'sensuous' Pure Land as we find described in the sūtra; he simply thought of it as a subordinate realm for those whose faith had not been perfected in this life. This he called the 'Transformed Pure Land' which was devised by the Buddha in order to lead his devotees to the 'True Pure Land' as complete Nirvāna. So, the 'Realm of Bliss' is not some kind of whimsical fantasy or imaginary tale. It is a real place where there is no suffering to be experienced and from which the attainment of true Buddha-hood can be attained with certainty (i.e., the non-retrogressive state). In the Transformed Pure Land, one also receives direct support from Amida Buddha in our journey towards perfect faith and liberation. For Shinran, however, the True Pure Land of Nirvāna is attainable immediately at the time of death for the person who has realised shinjin in this life (in other words, the non-retrogressive stage can be attained now). In this respect, he represents a radical shift from the tradition that preceded him.

So where does all this leave us? A resolution to the problem is to see, perhaps, the Transformed Pure Land as either the creation of the transcendental bodhisattva, Dharmākara, who generated the karmic merit necessary to establish this realm; or as a compassionate mani-festation of the True Pure Land itself. Similarly, one can view Amida Buddha as having emerged as a result of Dharmākara's aeons of spir-itual practice and who now presides in his glorious Land of Bliss; or you can see him as the personal face of Nirvāna, projected by the Dharma-Body itself, for the sake of suffering sentient beings. Differ-ent intellectual and affective temperaments will be drawn to either of these interpretations but both are acceptable positions in my view. What matters, ultimately, is our complete surrender to the inconceiv-able grace of Amida Buddha and our faith in his power to bring us to the Other Shore of Enlightenment.

It is important to establish our lives upon perfectly firm ground. Without a firm basis, all our efforts will be in vain. It is like doing acrobatics atop a cloud—an impossible feat: the performers are sure to fail. How can one attain that perfectly firm ground? We arrive at it only through an encounter with the Infinite.

Manshi Kiyozawa

APPENDIX

Selected Dharma Passages

Buddhism

The philosophical question is not how to be happy but *why* all beings want to be happy. All life, all existence, has only one aim and purpose, namely happiness. We are beings who crave happiness and abhor suffering, says the Buddha. And so we incessantly reflect on how we can become happy, and when we imagine that we have done so, we are anxious and troubled about remaining happy. . . . Why do we insist on being happy and feel that we are entitled to it as a right? Why does even the most miserable situation carry a gleam of hope? Because happiness is the state of our true nature, the condition of our real Self. The Self ever abides in the bliss of Nirvāna; all life outside its immediate sphere of influence is, relative to this bliss, suffering. . . . Indeed, we learn how to be cheerful only after we have discovered that life, as such, is sad.

P. J. SAHER

The ultimate end of Buddhism is to turn suffering into spiritual peace.

RYUKYO FUJIMOTO

It is a general Buddhist conviction that ordinary life is hopelessly unsatisfactory, exposed to constant pain and grief, and in any case quite futile, since death swallows all so soon. Without the Dharma, no lasting happiness is possible.

EDWARD CONZE

On the surface, we may believe that we can approach ultimate truth if we just follow the practices taught in the Buddhist tradition. But actually, the more we perform spiritual practices, the more entangled in our limitations we become. Then, the more we become aware of the depths of our unawareness, the more we realise how impotent we are to realise Awakening through our own efforts. Accordingly, although the ideal of aspiring to attain Buddhahood is very important, in reality, it is practically impossible.

Jōdo Shinshū: A Guide

If Buddhism has truth in it, and is a living religion full of vital power, it can neither remain as the Buddhism of meditation ... nor that of contemplation and commandments; it should not be confined to mountain recesses or secluded monasteries, to be monopolised by the choicest few. It must be active and effective in the grim realities of life; it should be practical and not merely the subject of scholarly speculation.

Kenshō Yokogawa

The Buddha does not demand any belief but only promises knowledge.

George Grimm

A Buddhist must live in two worlds at once. What are these two worlds? They are the supramundane world and the mundane world, the world of oneness and the world of diversity, the world of supreme truth and the world of common sense. These worlds may be described as the Absolute and the relative, or the Infinite and the finite.... Basically, the two most outstanding spiritual features of a Buddhist are: first, that he *mentally* transcends the world of diversity (or secularity) and enters the world of oneness (or supreme truth), from which point he views the world of diversity; and, second, that he *physically* stays in the world of diversity, from which point he views the world of oneness, while striving to liberate and benefit others.

Manshi Kiyozawa

However noble and lofty a teaching may be, it is of utterly no avail if it remains out of reach of the common people who remain trapped and continue to sink in the quagmire of samsāra.

Ryukyo Fujimoto

Once a man told Rennyo what was worrying him, saying 'My mind can be compared to pouring water into a basket. While I am in the congregation being preached to about Buddhism, I feel grateful and even awe-stricken. But right after that, I'm aware that I am no better than before'. Thereupon Rennyo said to him 'Sink the basket [that is your mind] into the Dharma'.

Goichidai-kikigaki

Selected Dharma Passages

If we think about it deeply, we may notice that life is simply an endless cycle of birth, suffering and death, and that most are simply engaged in a futile struggle not to die. Whatever our life span, we can choose either to resign ourselves to existing in the shadow of these inevitable truths, or to enjoy our lives to the fullest, with the confidence instilled by knowing the teaching of the Buddha. This existence is then enhanced by the brilliance of limitless life, in which death is merely a rite of passage.

Jōdo Shinshū: A Guide

If science surveys the objective world and philosophy unravels intricacies of logic, Buddhism dives into the very abyss of being and tells us, in the directest possible manner, all it sees under the surface.

D. T. Suzuki

Unlike official Christianity, Buddhism is not a historical religion and its message is valid independently of the historicity of any event in the life of the 'founder', who did not found anything but merely transmitted a Dharma pre-existing him from eternity.

Edward Conze

According to an error widespread in the West, the spiritual 'extinction' that Buddhism has in view is a 'nothingness', as if it were possible to realise something that is nothing. Now either Nirvāna is nothingness, in which case it is unrealisable, or else it is realisable, in which case it must correspond to something real.

Frithjof Schuon

Life is a never-ending concatenation of births and deaths. What Buddhist philosophy teaches is to see into the meaning of life as it flows on. When Buddhists declare that all things are impermanent, subject to conditions, and that there is nothing in this world of samsāra ('birth-and-death') which can give us hope for absolute security, they mean that, as long as we take this world of transiency as something worth clinging to, we are sure to lead a life of frustration.

D. T. Suzuki

We should understand, of course, that Buddhism is not primarily concerned with reforming the world. We do not hope to make this life a paradise on earth. Thus, the spirit of gratitude is not a means to an end. It is not by gratitude that we transcend life and attain Nirvāna. Gratitude is, rather, an indication of some degree of spiritual attainment.

Kōshō Ōtani

Buddhism provides a decisive argument against any science purporting to be an end in itself: namely, that the fact of becoming 'objectively' preoccupied with the phenomenal world inevitably draws us into a morass of conjectures and illusions, and therefore away from Deliverance. The wish for exactitude professed by this science is thus far from constituting a guarantee of intrinsic value and spiritual legitimacy. "They do not understand that the objective world derives from the Spirit itself"—says the *Lankāvatāra Sūtra*—"and do not grasp that the whole system of thought likewise derives from it; but attributing reality to these manifestations of the Spirit, they examine them, senseless people that they are, and get attached to dualities such as: 'this and that' or 'to be and not to be'—without perceiving that there is but a single Essence."

Frithjof Schuon

The Ganges River is stirred up by the tramping of horses and elephants, and disturbed by the movements of fish and turtles; but the river flows on, pure and undisturbed by such trifles. Buddha is like the great river. The fish and turtles of other teachings swim about in its depths and push against its current, but in vain. Buddha's Dharma flows on, pure and undisturbed.

The Teaching of Buddha

The Hīnayāna attracts by its pragmatic approach and its soberness, the Mahāyāna by the emotional warmth of its ethics and the colourfulness of its spiritual world. The Hīnayānin is like a vigorous man who, although tired from a long journey, is striding out under bright sunshine towards a distant goal which he wants to reach soon. The Mahāyānin resembles a mature man who, without haste, moves about in his spacious house to which portraits in dark colours on the walls and old books impart an occult atmosphere. He who wishes to join the former man will be called to take long strides and not to waste time. He who wants to join the Mahāyānin, however, will be invited by him for a discussion about the task of being human—and for a cup of tea.

HANS WOLFGANG SCHUMANN

Samsāra

Everything is changeable, everything appears and disappears; there is no blissful peace until one passes beyond the agony of life and death.

The Teaching of Buddha

Birth, old age and death; grief and despair; separation from friends; the company of those we dislike; the non-fulfillment of desires—all these attributes of existence are suffering. As long as they are not eradicated, life cannot be called really happy. But since they are inseparable from it, life must be considered as sorrowful.... Here one may object that, although existence is not sheer pleasure, it nevertheless keeps sufficient joy in store for a more positive assessment. In fact, the Buddha in no way denied pleasures and pleasant experiences. On the contrary, he viewed them as a fixed part of life which otherwise would not appear as enticing as it does. His criterion of judgement was much more profound: it is permanence which he made the yardstick of true happiness. Everything joyful and dear ends in suffering because it is transitory. It is a false happiness, for it has to be counterbalanced with sorrow and tears.

HANS WOLFGANG SCHUMANN

Ordinary observers ... see nothing but the impermanence, transiency or changeability of things and are unable to see eternity itself.

D. T. SUZUKI

The world is, indeed, like a dream and the treasures of the world are an alluring mirage. Like the apparent distances in a picture, things have no reality in themselves but are like a heat haze.

The Teaching of Buddha

Our universe: an endless phantasmagory made only by combinations of combinations of combinations of units finding quality and form through unimaginable affinities—now thickly massed in solid glooms; now palpitating in tremulosities of light and colour; always and everywhere grouped by some stupendous art into one vast mosaic of polarities. Yet each unit in itself is a complexity inconceiv-

Selected Dharma Passages

able, and each in itself also a symbol only, a character, a single ideograph of the undecipherable text of the Infinite Riddle.

LAFCADIO HEARN

Indeed, it is very difficult to understand the world as it is, for, although it seems true, it is not, and, although it seems false, it is not. Ignorant people cannot know the truth concerning the world.

The Teaching of Buddha

The relation of individuality to karma is well illustrated by the simile of electricity. Karma can be likened to the electric current and individuality to the light. The current and the light are both electrical: the former is invisible, while the latter is but an observable aspect of the former under particular circumstances. In like manner, each individual being is the visual form of his invisible karma.

NISHU UTSUKI

Do not grieve or lament. Have I not always told you that all things dear and pleasant are subject to change, loss and instability? How else could it be here? That which was born, has come into being, has been effected [by the deeds of previous births as a new form of existence] and is subject to decay—that this should not perish is impossible.

THE BUDDHA

The things of this samsaric world are all illusion, like a dream.
Wherever one looks, where is their substance?
Palaces built of earth, stone and wood,
Wealthy men endowed with food, dress and finery,
Legions of retainers who throng round the mighty—
These are like castles in the air, like rainbows in the sky.
And how deluded those who think of this as truth!
When uncles, nephews, brothers and sisters gather as kindred do,
When couples and children gather as families do,
When friends and neighbours gather in good fellowship—
These are like meetings of dream friends, like travellers sharing food with strangers.
And how deluded those who think of this as truth!

The Unhindered Path

This phantom body grown in uterine water from a union of seed and
blood—
Our habitual passions springing from the bad deeds of our past,
Our thoughts provoked by various apparitions—
All are like flowers in autumn, clouds across the sky.
How deluded . . . if you have thought of them as permanent.
The splendid plumage of the peacock with its many hues,
Our melodious words in which notes high and low are mingled,
The link of causes and effects which now have brought us here
together—
They are like the sound of echoes, the sport of a game of illusion.
Meditate on these and do not seize on them as truth!
Mists on a lake, clouds across a southern sky,
Spray blown by wind above the sea,
Lush fruits ripened by the summer sun—
In permanence they cannot last; in a trice they separate and fall away.
Meditate on their illusion and do not think of them as permanent!
                                   The Buddha's Law Among the Birds

That rebirth is unavoidable for the unliberated, does not imply that
the new form of existence must necessarily be a human one. On the
contrary, a human form of existence is considered quite rare and difficult to obtain. . . . An existence in human embodiment is certainly
not the highest but, in Buddhist opinion, is the most favourable one
for liberation. . . . therefore it is preferable to all other forms of
existence. . . . The form in which a being is reborn after death is not,
in the least, a matter of accident. The law of causation governs here as
it does in the physical world where every effect has its cause and corresponds with that cause.
                                   HANS WOLFGANG SCHUMANN

Why is life so illusory and miserable? In the theory of karma, it is
taught that the cardinal cause of our existence is Ignorance, from
which arise lust, anger and folly which fetter us to this existence.
While Christianity teaches that 'the wages of sin is death', Buddhism
professes that 'the wages of Ignorance is life'. To root out this Ignorance is to remove karma; that is, to deliver us from this suffering
world.
                                   NISHU UTSUKI

The rational person observes, in this sea of impermanence, various aspects of happiness—the play of children, the joy of youthful lovers, the pleasures of bodily lust, the delight of a mother in her child. He knows and hears the exultation, the cries of delight of all whose wishes have been fulfilled, but he also knows and hears the grief and wailing of parents at the death of their children, the suffering of the sick and needy, the despair of the poor and friendless, the anguish of the dying. None but the wise can know and understand these things. The average person *does not want to know them*. He removes from sight and hearing everything that might thwart his craving for pleasant sensations. He puts the poor in homes, the sick in hospitals, the insane in asylums and criminals in prison—so that he may enjoy undisturbed the illusions of a pleasurable world. He romanticises death, stifling with flowers the unpleasant odour of putrefaction. But does he lessen wretchedness by trying to cover it up, or reduce the sum of suffering by an effort to ignore it? Can anyone, knowing the abysses of life, expect to find happiness in it?

GEORGE GRIMM

Death

One cannot look directly at either the sun or death.

FRANÇOIS DE LA ROCHEFOUCAULD

It must be borne in mind that no problem of life can be correctly solved until its relation to death is seen clearly.... Indeed, life is observed most plainly when viewed standing on the threshold of death.

NISHU UTSUKI

We are beset by a very sea of suffering, the waves of which beat upon us in endless surges of pain and self-renewal. Everything the 'I' experiences changes continually into something else; there is no sensation of joy which does not pass away, no feeling of sorrow which does not recur with inevitable certainty. Every pleasure is shadowed—even while we enjoy it—by the knowledge that it, too, will fade with the passing of the object which caused it and will be replaced by suffering equally acute. The greatest suffering comes when the whole sensory world passes away from us—the moment of death. Then, truly, am I overcome with grief and sorrow—only to appear in a new form, exposed to new life, new sensations, new decrepitude, new dying. What person, understanding this merry-go-round of unending despair, does not wish to get out of it?

GEORGE GRIMM

In the Buddhist evaluation, one life is already suffering enough; how much more the multitude of lives which every being has to pass through. For with death, the Buddha proclaims, existence is by no means at an end. The death of an unliberated person is necessarily followed by their rebirth, in which the suffering of living and dying is repeated. To be born and to die and to be born again—this is the cycle of samsāra.... New deaths, new births, new suffering—these are the prospects. Yet the Buddha's teaching is no pessimism. As he also teaches the possibility of liberation from suffering, it distinctly bears an optimistic character.

HANS WOLFGANG SCHUMANN

Selected Dharma Passages

As long as they feel quite safe and happily alive, people are apt to imagine that they are even-minded about death and, in times of stress and worry, they may even look forward to it. When, however, actually faced with the immediate prospect of death, they easily come under the sway of the frantic 'will to live' which nature seems to have imparted to all living creatures. Their mood changes, a kind of panic comes over them, and they cannot help feeling that it is always just a bit too soon right now.

Edward Conze

Death is an everyday affair in this world; we see it in every direction and at every moment of life—there is nothing strange about it. But when a friend is taken from among us, the event assumes a thought-provoking aspect and makes us think of it as if it were a thing that never happened before and would never happen again. There is something absolutely unique and final about death. It takes our thoughts and feelings away from things worldly and material, and carries them out into another realm whose truth and reality appeals powerfully to our sensibility. All worldly considerations melt away and we are awakened from a long dream. It is as if cold water had been poured over our fervid forehead and a new order of realities now confronts us. After all, there is something of real value behind fleeting individual existences, and it is this that is real and eternally surviving. Our work, however humble, gains its meaning only when it is considered in connection with this reality.

The Eastern Buddhist

Our present life is a continuity of coming to be and passing away. . . . Rebirth after death is like the lighting of one flame from another; nothing concrete passes over; there is continuity but not sameness.

Ananda Coomaraswamy

People are saying these days that many are dying because of pestilence. However, it is not because of pestilence that people die but because birth is the promise of death. Therefore, do not be surprised by death.

Rennyo

If a shock is the sudden annihilation of a part of what we think belongs to us, then death is the greatest shock of all. . . . Death means that craving is finally parted from its wealth, forced to give it up, and to let it go, because . . . the real home and resting-place of our spirit has remained unrealised. We die because we missed that possibility. It is therefore right that we should not only fear death but also be ashamed of it, as the silent witness to the fact that we have failed to arrive at our true destiny. Death is the price the individual pays for the separation and isolation which is born of ignorance and, at the same time, it is the supreme lesson in renunciation.

EDWARD CONZE

All Buddhists view life as illusory, transitory and miserable. Not that they are pessimists without rhyme or reason; they look at the misery, not only of the poor, but also of those who live in the lap of luxury. It is true that happiness and pleasure occasionally come to entertain us—at least so we hope. Unfortunately, however, it is also true that the dark side usually overbalances the bright, and that nothing happy and pleasurable remains as long as is desired. Any attempt to oppose this fact is but mere eulogy and a vain toil. Life is like a panorama and comes to an end at death.

NISHU UTSUKI

As a budding mushroom shoots upwards carrying soil on its head, so beings from their birth onwards carry decay and death along with them. For death has come together with birth, because everyone who is born must certainly die. Therefore this living being, from the time of their birth onwards, moves in the direction of death, without turning back even for a moment; just as the sun, once it has arisen, goes forward in the direction of its setting, and does not turn back for a moment on the path it traverses; or as a mountain stream rapidly tears down on its way, flows and rushes along, without turning back even for a moment. To one who goes along like that, death is always near; just as brooks get extinguished when dried up by the summer heat, as fruits are bound to fall from a tree early one day when their stalks have been rotted away by the early morning mists; as earthenware breaks when hit with a hammer; and as dewdrops are dispersed when touched by the rays of the sun. Thus death, like a murderer with a drawn sword, has come together with birth. Like the murderer who has raised his sword to our neck, so it deprives us of life. And there is no chance that it might desist.

BUDDHAGHOSA

If we are to avoid the assumption that our deep-seated longing for immortality has no prospect of fulfillment, then we are left with only one way out of the difficulty; namely, that death fundamentally does not touch us at all.... We can speak of immortality only so long as *something* in us does not change, even in death.

P.J. SAHER

Human Nature

Human desires are endless. It is like the thirst of a man who drinks salt water: he gets no satisfaction and his thirst is only increased.

Teaching of Buddha

We have no more say in the duration of our passions than in that of our lives.... In the human heart, new passions are forever being born; the overthrow of one almost always means the rise of another.

FRANÇOIS DE LA ROCHEFOUCAULD

Are we not often preaching the path of morality while inwardly consulting our own interests? Do we not often make a show of wisdom, while ignorant at heart? Isn't 'Peace!' on the lips of every nation, yet does ever a day pass without seeing nations struggle with each other? What calmness and resignation can science give us, whose basis is but hypotheses? Considering these things, we cannot but come to the conclusion that it is only by Amitābha's Vow and Name that we can be saved.

Synopsis of the Jōdo Shinshū Creed

What, after all, is the nature of this happiness which all so assiduously pursue? Is it something constant which, once overtaken, can be firmly anchored and confidently enjoyed, or does it not rather show itself as an insubstantial, elusive thing, one which already, even in the act of trying to perpetuate its savour in the mind, is beginning to dissolve away under one's perception of it, leaving behind only the aftertaste of regret? Youth turns, first imperceptibly and then at an accelerated pace, to age; and good health, however carefully conserved, must yet, before very long, yield before the onset of decrepitude, disease and death: this fact alone makes nonsense of the boastful claims to have extended human life thanks to medical research; for were the span of life to be prolonged by a hundred, two hundred, even a thousand years, would this make death, when it came, any more welcome? Or would it cause a person to use his life with greater mindfulness?

MARCO PALLIS

Selected Dharma Passages

The course of our moral lives never runs smoothly. The more conscientiously we try to realise good, the more elevated it appears to become, leaving us somewhere far below. The more we strive to be kind to others, the more keenly are we awakened to the self-love that asserts itself within and without.

RYUKYO FUJIMOTO

However deep your knowledge of abstruse philosophy, it is like a piece of hair placed in the vastness of space; and however important your experience of things worldly, it is like a drop of water thrown into an unfathomable abyss.

TE-SHAN

Generally speaking, we may judge people by their desires and divide them into three groups: (1) those who only feather their nests at the sacrifice of others; (2) those who are satisfied with themselves, neither injuring nor benefiting others; and (3) those who sacrifice themselves for the sake of all mankind.

SHŪGAKU YAMABE

All the time we seek to realise an absolute permanence and ease in this world. No limit can be discovered to our ambitions for a permanence which we persist in building on the shifting sands of time— through our children, through fame and 'lasting' achievements, through far-flung illusions of personal immortality, and so on. Similarly, a desire for an absolute ease seems to be behind our constant endeavours to make ourselves at home in this world, and to attain the kind of fool-proof happiness that is known as 'security'.

EDWARD CONZE

It is not that I don't understand today's intellectuals, who think religion is irrelevant and has no meaning for our daily lives. However, our everyday lives are floating, not securely grounded. And it is true religion that grounds a floating life.

DAIEI KANEKO

The Unhindered Path

All beings, and primarily all human beings, are in a desperate and hopeless state. Indeed, they are infinitely far removed from a state that is *perfectly* adequate to them. But just such a state is earnestly desired by every being as the highest goal, and the longing for it is the *primary* longing of everything that lives. Yet the fulfillment of this longing of all beings must be possible. In fact, nature always attains with certainty the ends she has striven after in the impulses of her beings. It is true that nature is not all powerful but she is all competent. Thus it is certain that, in beings, there must also be found the capacity and ability to satisfy their greatest longing.

GEORGE GRIMM

Contradiction is so deep-seated in life that it can never be eradicated until life is surveyed from a point higher than itself.

D. T. SUZUKI

According to the Buddhist, the highest moral feelings survive races, suns and universes. The purely unselfish feelings, impossible to grosser natures, belong to the Absolute. In generous natures the divine becomes sentient, quickens within the shell of illusion, as a child quickens in the womb. In yet higher natures, the feelings which are not of self find room for powerful manifestation and shine through the phantom-ego, as light through a vase. Such are purely unselfish love, larger than individual being, supreme compassion and perfect benevolence: they are not of man, but of the Buddha within man. And as these expand, all the feelings of self begin to thin and weaken. The condition of the phantom-ego simultaneously purifies: all those opacities which darkened the reality of Mind, within the mirage of mind, begin to illumine; and the sense of the infinite, like a thrilling of light, passes through the dream of personality into the awakening divine.

LAFCADIO HEARN

It would be quite wrong to interpret the doctrine of karma along deterministic lines. Only the quality, that is the social surrounding, the physical appearance and the mental abilities of a person are fixed by the deeds of their previous existences, but in no way their actions.

Selected Dharma Passages

The Buddha took it for granted that the innate character of each being leaves them the freedom to decide the actions which determine their future.

HANS WOLFGANG SCHUMANN

The ordinary man who repeats the vicious cycle of delusion, karma and pain because of his spiritual darkness, tries to cling to things with the thought that they exist firmly and that they are worth striving for. When the Buddha said, 'All things are transient', he meant that all existing things, including ourselves, are in constant flux and that things and persons dear to us soon pass away. . . . By thus disclosing the painful aspects of life and the world, the Buddha leads us to aspire for the state of ultimate tranquility (*Nirvāna*) in which no passions arise and no delusion gives rise to further karmic commotions which entail pain. Since the cause of our suffering is ignorance and passions which are inherent in ourselves, to get rid of the cause of this suffering means to put an end to our own existence, together with all the karmic tendencies which continue to work, even after our physical death, to produce a new life.

HISAO INAGAKI

A genuinely carefree attitude, a serene outlook; these are not to be won by refusing to face facts, and it is rather those who, despite all warnings, insist on laying up their treasure where moth and rust will corrupt it who, as the inescapable hour of disappointment draws near, will yield to despair. Clutching hard at things which, in the very course of nature are bound to disappear, they try to put off the hour of awareness, using every possible narcotic device that human ingenuity can invent, the true 'opium of the people'; but, despite their efforts, they are overtaken by fate and certainly their end will be a lamentable one.

MARCO PALLIS

The Buddha's great message is that *everything* cognisable is frail, perishable and thus ultimately sorrowful. Consequently our true Self can be satisfied only by something that is imperishable and thus without sorrow. When we grasp this, there comes peace which is always followed by happiness.

P.J. SAHER

A man who chases after fame, wealth and love affairs is like a child who licks honey from the blade of a knife.

The Teaching of Buddha

We may talk about transcending the cycle of birth-and-death but, when we try to do it, we find it is impossible. It is our nature to cling to our lives, even when inflicted with a fatal illness and, no matter how old we get, we do not wish to die. How can we, who are always caught up in personal obligations and kindnesses, be freed from feelings of love and hate? Intellectuals, who look down on the illiterate, find, ultimately, that their knowledge is unreliable and useless. And the so-called foolish have the same worries as the well-educated. Either way, we cannot separate ourselves from this, our worldly living.

Daiei Kaneko

So long as our hearts are bent upon external pleasures, or are in dependence upon material things, there is no true happiness or peace of mind. Anguish seizes us and we find ourselves forlorn and hopeless.

William McGovern

If a dry bone is smeared with blood, a dog will gnaw at it until he is tired and frustrated. Lust to a man is precisely like this bone to a dog; he will covet it until he is exhausted.

The Teaching of Buddha

Whatever kind of life we may lead, for each of us there is only this one brief period of time—our irreplaceable human life. Yet, what if, when our life was about to come to an end, we were left with only such futile thoughts as 'Why was I alive? What was the purpose of my life?' How pitiable we would be if, at our death, we were left with only feelings of regret, resentment and remorse. Wouldn't we want to live so that, at our death, we could quietly reflect upon our lives, saying 'In my life there have been some sad and bitter times but how grateful I am to have lived such a life, in which I have been able to encounter the Buddha of Unlimited Life'?

Jitsuen Kakehashi

Selected Dharma Passages

When we reflect deeply, we encounter the sorrowful contradiction that, while working hard to live, we are marching onward to the grave. We often wonder whose trick it is that makes us long for eternal life when life is so transient.

Synopsis of the Jōdo Shinshū Creed

The person who hankers for permanent possession of an impermanent object is, simply, a fool: in any case, the intelligent person does not protract his desire beyond the natural life of its object and does not therefore suffer greatly at the object's passing. He wastes neither time nor energy in grief but calms himself by looking directly and fearlessly at the facts of life.

P. J. SAHER

In this finite life of ours, the wall of holiness is altogether too high for us to scale successfully and, if this were made the only condition by which we were allowed to be saved, there would indeed be very few mortals on the topmost rung of the ladder.

GESSHŌ SASAKI

Only when we are shone upon from the outside and view ourselves mirrored in that light—only then, for the first time, are we able to see a complete picture of ourselves. The light of the Buddha's higher wisdom alone reaches to the very base of our being; it allows us to see our delusion for what it is. This is because the Buddha's higher wisdom enters us fully and opens our hearts.

Jōdo Shinshū: A Guide

Shinran's teaching must be regarded as the direct communication of Amida Buddha which, on the one hand, dispels the darkness of this defiled world by means of the pure light of wisdom and, on the other, gives the necessary moisture by sending down the spiritual rain of nectar, to us who are ignorant, confused and dying of dryness of heart.

KAKUNYO

The Dharma-Body

The Dharma-Body (*Dharmakāya*) is the substance of the Dharma; that is, of the Truth itself. In the aspect of Essence, Buddha has no shape or colour and, since Buddha has no shape or colour, he comes from nowhere and there is nowhere for him to go. Like the blue sky, he arches over everything, and since he is all things, he lacks nothing.

The Teaching of Buddha

The doctrine of the Dharmakāya arose from the deep longing which the disciples of Shakyamuni felt after the passing of the Master. They believed that the true body of the Buddha was above birth and death. The Buddha told them, 'I pass away but the Dharmakāya of the Tathāgata remains forever'.

Beatrice Lane Suzuki

The Absolute, the Universal Buddha or the Essence of Mind is the supreme ideal which is behind all life and from which all things draw their sustenance.

William McGovern

The Dharmakāya is the immanent as well as transcendent truth or reality of all beings and appearances: the indestructible, timeless Absolute, the one essence in and behind all that was, is and will be. It is the bearer and object of enlightenment.

Hans Wolfgang Schumann

Since Buddha-nature is Tathāgata or Dharmakāya, the ultimate level of understanding, then Buddha-nature is a term used to refer to the ultimate with the reference being sentient beings. This same ultimate … is Amida, so Amida acting within sentient beings is Buddha-nature. Finally, Buddha-nature is *shinjin*. Speaking more abstractly, one could say that Dharmakāya, when seen from the vantage point of sentient beings is called Buddha-nature and, speaking more conventionally, Amida's compassion extended to sentient beings is called *shinjin*. These two statements are the same.

Jōdo Shinshū: A Guide

Selected Dharma Passages

If the element of the Buddha did not exist in everyone, there would be no disgust with suffering, nor could there be a wish for Nirvāna, nor striving for it, nor a resolve to win it.

Ratnagotravibhāga

The principle of Suchness is not static; it is full of dynamic forces.

D.T. SUZUKI

Within every creature ... sleeps the Infinite Intelligence: unevolved, hidden, unfelt, unknown, yet destined from all eternity to waken at last, to rend away the ghostly web of sensuous mind, to break forever its chrysalis of flesh, and pass to the supreme conquest of space and time.

LAFCADIO HEARN

The work of Buddha is to manifest, in all affairs and on all occasions, the pure essence of Dharmakāya (the absolute nature of Buddha); so Buddha's mercy and compassion flow out from this Dharmakāya in endless life and boundless light, bringing salvation to mankind.

The Teaching of Buddha

The Dharma-Body is eternal, immutable and omnipresent; it acts without interruption everywhere and its activities never come to an end as long as there are beings to be saved.... It transcends not only all thought but also all karma and causality.... The Dharma-Body is unconditioned because it is not conditioned by karma and passions; it is not unconditioned because it has the sovereign power to manifest itself as something conditioned, and does so repeatedly.

EDWARD CONZE

The Buddha's body fills every corner of the universe; it reaches everywhere and exists forever, regardless of whether people believe in him or doubt his existence.

The Teaching of Buddha

The Unhindered Path

The Absolute is the ocean and life's phenomena the waves. The ocean is always changing. Waves are constantly arising and while no two waves are alike, they are all of the same essence—water—and the essence remains unchanged, though it is constantly assuming new and different shapes and transformations. So does the stream of life ever go surging past, never remaining the same. Yet there is a certain stability, a fixity, a changelessness in this very changeability.... In like manner, says the Mahāyāna, does the Absolute express itself in the Universe without in the least affecting its own essence. It is the Eternal Being and yet the Eternal Becoming. Furthermore, as there can be an ocean without waves but no waves without an ocean so, the Mahāyāna declares, no life would be possible without having, for its essence, this reality.

WILLIAM MCGOVERN

Just as pieces of various kinds of pottery are of the same nature in that they are made of clay, so the various magic-like manifestations (*māyā*) of both enlightenment and non-enlightenment are aspects of the same essence, Suchness.

The Awakening of Faith in the Mahāyāna

Shakyamuni Buddha boldly proclaimed that the Dharma was not something that he had arbitrarily created himself. It had always existed and would continue to exist. It had nothing to do with whether he was born in this world or not. All he had done was to experience that Dharma in order to expound it for the sake of others. What allowed Shakyamuni to become a Buddha is the reality of the Dharma. This is referred to as *Dharmakāya* ('Dharma-Body') which is the body of ultimate reality and transcendent truth; it is beyond both time and space, yet immanent in the world.

Jōdo Shinshū: A Guide

The only reality is One—all that we have taken for substance is only shadow. The physical is the unreal and the outer man is the ghost.

LAFCADIO HEARN

Selected Dharma Passages

The true nature of the Dharmakāya is a real substance with which we can unite, a substance that is true and permanent. . . . When we are enlightened, the Dharmakāya is found not to be empty but active, and we understand the meaning of the true teaching of non-ego that is emptiness of the small self but not of the Great Self. . . . In Nirvāna, the self enlarges to become one with all other selves and true individuality is not lost. Each individual becomes the centre of the universe, but we must realise that all other beings are ourselves. . . .

We must not cling to the small self but enlarge it to contain all others. This constitutes the real self and the knowledge of it is Nirvāna that is full of bliss.

Great enlightenment is tranquil, bright and filled with compassion for all beings. . . . It is the teaching of non-duality, of Buddha-nature, of enlightenment, of union with the One that brings the vision of truth and insight into reality. . . . The whole trouble with us unenlightened beings is that we regard ourselves as separate when, in reality, we are united in the Dharmakāya. This is the true meaning of 'non-ego'.

BEATRICE LANE SUZUKI

The Universal Buddha is far more than the sum-total of existence. Its essence remains unchanged throughout all eternity, and the basic nature of one phenomenon is exactly the same as another, though the mode of expression or manifestation may be widely different. . . . The Universe is but a mode of the Universal.

WILLIAM McGOVERN

In Buddhist Emptiness, there is no time, no space, no becoming, 'nothing-ness'; it is what makes all things possible; it is a zero full of infinite possibilities, it is a void of inexhaustible contents.

D.T. SUZUKI

The Absolute, the philosophical principle behind the world, is identical with the principle of religious salvation, with Buddhahood or the personal Buddha. The Supreme Buddha pervades the entire universe and is present in everything. Each thought, sound and action is, in its true essence, an activity of his saving grace. As a manifestation of the

The Unhindered Path

Absolute, this very world contains all the mysteries of reality and its hidden forces can be used for salvation. As a reflex of the Non-dual, it must everywhere mirror, manifest and reveal this all-comprehensive unity. If all things are fundamentally identical in one Pure Spirit, all cosmic phenomena can be conceived of as closely linked together by many invisible threads, with each word, action and thought being somehow connected with the eternal Ground of the world.

EDWARD CONZE

The karma-ego we call *self* is our mind and body; both perpetually decay, both are perpetually renewed. From the unknown beginning, this double phenomenon, objective and subjective, has been alternately dissolved and integrated: each integration is a birth; each dissolution a death. There is no other birth or death but the birth and death of karma in some form or condition. But at each rebirth, the reintegration is never that of the identical phenomenon but of another, to which it gives rise, as growth begets growth, as motion produces motion. So that the phantom-self changes, not only as to form and condition, but as to actual personality with every re-embodiment. There is one Reality; but there is no permanent individual, no constant personality: there is only the phantom-self, and phantom succeeds to phantom, as undulation to undulation, over the ghostly sea of birth-and-death. And even as ... it is the form of the wave only, not the wave itself, that travels, so in the passing of lives there is only the rising and the vanishing of forms; forms mental, forms material. The fathomless Reality does not pass.

LAFCADIO HEARN

The myriad changes and transformations of all existing things in the universe are the wondrous working of one great, inconceivable power.

MANSHI KIYOZAWA

This absolute reality, the very point of rest in the universe, is our eternal destination.

GEORGE GRIMM

Selected Dharma Passages

The Formless, the Eternal, the Boundless, the Universal is manifested as the Supreme Person. Amida was such a personification in the enlightened spiritual consciousness of Shakyamuni. The Dharmakāya, which is beyond description and without attributes, revealed itself as Amida, the Spirit of Joy . . . to whom all personalities are related.

KENRYO KANAMATSU

Shinran's view of 'oneness' is not that of a static ultimate reality which penetrates all beings in the universe, but of a dynamic working of the ultimate. . . . Oneness, which is formless and colourless, manifests itself in form and colour—namely, as Amida and his Pure Land.

MICHIO TOKUNAGA

Nirvāna

There is a world which is not of this world, though inseparable from it . . . a world of lights not accompanied by any form of shade.

D. T. SUZUKI

Nirvāna, as the true Reality, is one and it has no second. All multiplicity, all separation, all duality is a sign of falseness. Everything apart from the One, also called 'Emptiness' or 'Suchness', is devoid of real existence and whatever may be said about it is ultimately untrue, false and nugatory, though perhaps permissible if the salvation of beings requires it. The ability to frame salutary statements and to act in conformity with people's needs, springs from a faculty called 'skill-in-means' (*upāya*).

EDWARD CONZE

Nirvāna has four characteristics: (i) permanence (of the Absolute); (ii) bliss (in the awareness of one's identity with it); (iii) freedom (from bondage to sorrowful things); and (iv) purity (of emotions and craving).

HANS WOLFGANG SCHUMANN

Absolute Nirvāna is synonymous with the Dharmakāya. It is eternally immaculate in its essence and constitutes the truth and reality of all existence. Though it manifests itself in the world of defilement and relativity, its essence remains forever undefiled. . . . It is universally present in all beings and makes their existence real.

Vijñānamātra Sāstra

We are beings who cannot detach ourselves from anxieties and suffering. The realm without anxiety and suffering is called the Pure Land or the realm of Nirvāna, which means quietude and stillness; it is a place without disturbance and conflict. There are no discriminations based on love and hate, and the defilements of worldly desires are absent. But in the midst of this life of anxiety and suffering, we do not doubt the existence of the realm of Nirvāna. Thus, as Shinran said, 'though the light of the sun is veiled by clouds and mist, beneath them there is still brightness'.

DAIEI KANEKO

Nirvāna is nothing other than the highest culmination of love. It is the absolute dying to the self which is, at once, the absolute rebirth of the self in the Universal Self.

KENRYO KANAMATSU

When Faith is awakened in the minds of deluded and defiled ordinary people, they are made aware that 'birth-and-death is Nirvāna'.

SHINRAN

It is not the sentient and conscious self that enters Nirvāna. The ego is only a temporary aggregate of countless illusions, a bubble sure to break. It is a creation of karma, or rather, it *is* karma. Acts and thoughts are forces integrating themselves into material and mental phenomena, into what we call objective and subjective appearances. The very earth we tread on, the mountains and forests, the rivers and seas, the world and its moon, the visible universe in short, *is the integration of acts and thoughts*, is karma or, at least, reality conditioned by karma.

LAFCADIO HEARN

Nirvāna is an 'invisible infinite consciousness, which shines everywhere' (*Dīghanikāya*)—the non-impermanent centre of the personality which constitutes an absolute element in this contingent world.

EDWARD CONZE

I shall go to the motionless, to the unshakable, with which nothing can be compared.

Sutta Nipāta

The striving for Nirvāna is a perpetual struggle between false and true, light and darkness, the sensual and the super-sensual; and the ultimate victory can be gained only by the total decomposition of the mental and physical individuality. Not one conquest of self can suffice: millions of selves must be overcome. For the false ego is a compound of countless ages, possessing a vitality enduring beyond universes. At each breaking and shedding of the chrysalis, a new one appears; more tenuous, perhaps, more diaphanous but woven of like sensuous material; a mental and physical texture spun by karma from the inherited illusions, passions, desires, pains and pleasures, of innumerable lives.

LAFCADIO HEARN

A popular Japanese saying is that 'those who have passed away are all buddhas'. This may make you think that the number of buddhas is immeasurable; however, they are simply going back to one, Amida Buddha. Because of that, while reciting the nembutsu, we are made to feel that we are talking with our loved ones. This realm is called 'Great Nirvāna', which is what we long for as our spiritual home; it is where all human karmic sufferings and blind passions cease—it feels so warm and dear to us, doesn't it? In that place, where all anxieties are extinguished, we feel and sense the truth that is never extinguished.

DAIEI KANEKO

In Māhāyana Buddhism, Nirvāna is positive, not negative; in other words, the finding of the real, the true Self. It is the ending of woe and ignorance. Enlightenment discloses the true reality which is non-ego in the true sense, in which every notion of separation is done away with and true unity prevails. *Attā*, the ego, is impermanent; the permanent is Nirvāna.

BEATRICE LANE SUZUKI

Buddha-Nature

Buddha-nature exists in everyone no matter how deeply it may be covered over by greed, anger and foolishness, or buried by their own deeds and retribution. Buddha-nature cannot be lost or destroyed; when all defilements are removed, sooner or later it will reappear. . . . Buddha-nature is not something that comes to an end. Though wicked men should be born as beasts or hungry demons, or fall into hell, they never lose their Buddha-nature. . . . The diamond, the hardest of known substances, cannot be crushed. Sand and stones can be ground to powder but diamonds remain unscathed. Buddha-nature is like a diamond, and thus cannot be broken.

The Teaching of Buddha

All sentient beings possess Buddha-nature. Ordinary, unenlightened people are not able to see that all sentient beings possess it. How can their minds, which see oneself as good and others as bad, know that all sentient beings possess Buddha-nature? But just as parents do not see any bad children, in the eyes of [Amida Buddha], beings without Buddha-nature simply do not exist, and this is not just because we are seen by the Buddha's compassion but because we are also seen, through and through, by the Buddha's wisdom.

DAIEI KANEKO

It is the underlying unity, the quintessence of all being. It is the eternal sameness underlying all apparent difference. Owing to our subjective activity, we build up a vision of a discrete, particularised universe but, in reality, the essence of things ever remains one, void of particularity.

WILLIAM MCGOVERN

To know the difference between the real Self and the ego is to have grasped the Buddha's idea of *anattā*. . . . Our true Self is unimaginable, inconceivable, indescribable and unfathomable. . . . If this Self lies beyond the phenomenal world, then it also lies beyond the transitory. . . . Hence the Self also lies beyond that which brings sorrow.

GEORGE GRIMM

Non-ego does indeed deny the possibility of identifying man's spirit with the impermanent elements of his being, but not with the permanent elements which are of the same essence as the Dharmakāya. Is not this the best kind of immortality?

BEATRICE LANE SUZUKI

The Māhāyana came to the conclusion that it is really the Buddha in us who does the seeking and that it is the Buddha-nature in us which seeks Buddhahood.

EDWARD CONZE

Amida Buddha

As a representation of the *Dharmakāya*, Amida's light shines unhindered throughout the universe. All beings are touched by this light. It is the light of his Primal Vow. Thus, we come to realise that the highest reality of non-duality, which manifests as Amida Buddha, also includes us. This leads one to understand that there is no path to follow or practice to cause one's awakening. What can we do if there is no practice that can be performed to experience true entrusting? The only way is to 'listen', which means to be open and free from conditioning.

Jōdo Shinshū: A Guide

Amida as Dharmakāya is always eternal . . . viewed from its phase of *prajñā* (Wisdom); but, viewed from the aspect of *mahā-karuna* or Great Compassion, Amida is the Tathāgata who ever goes out into samsāra and ever returns to *tathātā* (Suchness) in constant succession for the sake of liberating humanity.

Ryukyo Fujimoto

The delusion of human existence is the very reason for Amida's mind flowing into it.

Michio Tokunaga

Amida, leaving the evil nature of sentient beings as it is, gives them his good mind; not that he destroys their nature and replaces it by a new one made solely of the Buddha's wisdom.

Rennyo

Our inmost longing is to become immortal, to attain eternal life. In this very longing of ours, Amida too longs. It is the Absolute and Eternal Life which possesses—and is—the True World, that inspires this very longing.

Kenryo Kanamatsu

Amida is 'Infinite Light' and, therefore, there is no corner of the human heart where his rays do not penetrate: he is 'Eternal Life' and, therefore, there is not a moment in our lives when he is not urging us to rise above ourselves. His vows reflect his will—a will illumined by Infinite Light and imbued with Eternal Life; they cannot be otherwise than the most efficient cause to lift us above ourselves who are limited individuals in time and space.

D.T. SUZUKI

Amida Buddha, as Shinran conceived and perceived him, is thus universally resplendent, of the nature of Wisdom, omnipresent and active. But Amida, having these characteristics, is not merely an object of awe, worship and reverence, but his Light of Wisdom and Compassion embraces and encompasses us, pierces through the hard core of self-attachment and ignorance, and gives us the meaning of life and the world.

HISAO INAGAKI

Amida . . . is nothing but an event in the realm of the eternal Dharmakāya. Amida, in time, is a personification of the Dharmakāya and, in space, Amida consummated the Land of Bliss; and, yet, he himself is the eternal and universal Dharmakāya which is beyond time and space.

RYUKYO FUJIMOTO

Our hearts and minds are brutalised by our efforts to get by in everyday life; our awareness of the truth is obstructed by our ignorance and base passions. Therefore, we cannot see the figure of Amida Buddha, yet we are always enveloped by the light of Great Compassion and protected by it.

Jōdo Shinshū: A Guide

An expression of the 'personal reality' of the Buddha is the saving invocation of the name of Amitābha and . . . the sacramental image of the Tathāgata—true 'manifestation of the Void' (*sūnyamūrti*) and 'expression of the inexpressible'.

FRITHJOF SCHUON

The power of Tathāgata is unsurpassed. The power of Tathāgata is omnipresent. It pervades everything and works freely, without hindrance. By committing myself to the wondrous power of Tathāgata, I have great peace and comfort. By entrusting the great question of life and death to Tathāgata, I have no fear, no discontentment.

MANSHI KIYOZAWA

The God of Christianity is one of love and justice, while Amida Buddha is mercy itself and nothing more. In the world, the principle of karma prevails and the Buddha never judges. The God of Judaism was represented by Christ to be the God of love, yet he is made to judge our sins and mete out punishments accordingly. Amida, however, knows only infinite love for all beings, wishing to deliver them from the eternal cycle of ignorance and suffering in which they are found migrating. In Amida, therefore, there is no wrath, no hatred, no jealousy.

SHŪGAKU YAMABE

Amitābha is absolute compassion that, in conformity with the truth, breaks down obstinate selfishness and loves ignorant and bewildered people, equally and universally, without any distinction of person.

Synopsis of the Jōdo Shinshū Creed

Without knowing I am already embraced, I ignorantly resist the Compassionate hands.

TAKEKO KUJO

Our true self is nothing but this: committing our total existence to the wondrous working of the Infinite, then settling down just as we are. Once the commitment to the Infinite is made, life and death are no longer of concern. If even life and death are no longer of concern, then surely there is no need to worry about things of lesser importance.

MANSHI KIYOZAWA

When Shinran speaks of the oneness of the Buddha's body and the Buddha's land, it means that the state of those who are born in that land, and Amida Buddha's state of being, are identical.

DAIEI KANEKO

The Unhindered Path

Amida is the self-manifestation of Absolute Oneness or the dynamic display of the 'True Void'.

KENSHŌ YOKOGAWA

Normally, when we call someone, they will answer. We think that's the way it is with the Buddha also. But it isn't so. The Buddha calls us first. The only problem is that we do not hear his voice and keep wandering in this world.

JIKAI FUJIYOSHI

Although we are reluctant to approach the Buddha, he, out of Great Compassion, approaches us and enters into our minds. Amida's Light has this power, awakening us to reality—the reality of our existence—and giving us true joy and happiness. Amida as such is the Great Consoler of those who are lost in the forest of miseries and suffering. He removes our doubt and anxiety, and establishes in our minds Faith that is pure, joyful and resolute.

HISAO INAGAKI

Amitābha is Light in space while Amitāyus is Life in time, so Amida is master of space and time and, through him, we transcend both.

BEATRICE LANE SUZUKI

The light of Amida Buddha is surpassingly good; it is luminous and wondrous among all that is good. It is pleasing beyond compare and boundlessly excellent. Amida Buddha's light is pure, without the least defilement or diminution. Amida Buddha's light is superbly beautiful, a hundred million times more brilliant than the sun and the moon.

Sūtra of Salvation through the Perfect Enlightenment of Amida, Supreme among Buddhas

The Pure Land

Even when, judging from our own ignorant condition, we imagine ourselves happy, we may be deceiving ourselves; for, in the Buddha's eyes, our apparent happiness may really be pain. In such a world of impurity as this, it is impossible to find a true state of peace and happiness. Fame, wealth, love, learning—these are ever leading us downward into an abyss of utter darkness. Where can we find a region that harbours no pain? There stands Amida pointing to his Land of Purity and Happiness, where our worldly sufferings and tribulations are no more. In this land, there always smiles the spring of peace. No pain but all beauty, goodness and joy. Those born there enjoy a happiness that knows no ending; they are endowed not only with infinite wisdom and liberty, but with pure love and compassion which has the power to save all beings from the world of pain. All this happiness enjoyed by those who are in the Pure Land is the outcome of Amida's love and will to save.

Principal Teachings of the True Sect of Pure Land

It is undeniable, for those who are versed in Buddhism, that the Pure Land described in the *Larger Sūtra* is the realm of Nirvāna. Shakyamuni therein extends the positive aspects of Nirvāna to encompass Immortality, Serenity, Peace, Felicity, Truth, Purity, Liberation, the Transcendent and the Imperishable.

RYUKYO FUJIMOTO

Contrary to the Pure Land teaching, there is a teaching for sages, which says that the true aspect of this world must be the Pure Land or that we must actualise the Pure Land in this world. This idea is well accepted by today's intellectuals. But from the standpoint of the Pure Land way, this is nothing but the human idealisation of the Tathāgata's Primal Vow. As an idea, it seems to be close to us but it is so very far from reality. On the contrary, expecting the Pure Land of Nirvāna in the coming life is an idea that seems far away but, in reality, it is the closest to us. When we try to create the Pure Land in this world, the Pure Land goes away; and when we expect the Pure Land in the next life, the light of the Pure Land comes close to us and illumines this world. This is an inconceivable truth.

DAIEI KANEKO

The Unhindered Path

One aspect of being born in the Pure Land is that it is a terminus for our negative characteristics and resulting karmic suffering. The other aspect, however, is that it allows us to attain limitless life and higher wisdom. It enables us to work as a bodhisattva for the benefit of all sentient beings, endlessly into the future.

Jōdo Shinshū: A Guide

In the heavens, the principal reason for receiving pleasures is to develop an antipathy towards them; while, in the Pure Land, one may enjoy various pleasures and yet not form an attachment to them. Furthermore, in the Pure Land, there also exists the pleasure of hearing and practicing the teachings of the Buddha while, in the heavens, such a pleasure does not exist.

Buddhism and Jōdo Shinshū

The identification of rebirth [in the Pure Land] with Enlightenment is a unique doctrine of the Shin teachings. Through it, death loses its terror because the hope of rebirth has taken its place and motivates our daily life. The end of this life is the dawn of eternal life, eternal peace and eternal joy.

Kōshō Ōtani

That pure and beautiful land of happiness is for us; Amida, wishing to have us join him in the Pure Land, is ever showering his light upon us in order to make us grow in wisdom and become conscious of our ... falsehood whereby we might come to entertain the desire of being born in the land of truth and goodness.

Principal Teachings of the True Sect of Pure Land

The Pure Land is an infinite world and this world a finite one. Therefore, through the eyes of Buddha, this world, where ordinary, unenlightened people live, must also be Buddha's realm. In the eyes of ordinary people, however, the Pure Land exists beyond this world and is therefore a place to be longed for. But even that longing is made possible because the infinite permeates the finite. Ordinary, unenlightened beings long for the Pure Land of Nirvāna because the

Selected Dharma Passages

Tathāgata endows them with the entrusting mind. And with this realisation, we see that the reason we do not identify ourselves with the Buddha is due to the very human realisation that we are not enlightened.

DAIEI KANEKO

If the Land of Purity and Bliss were not a realm that is essentially *Sūnyatā*, then it would have to be regarded as a world of devas or as some sort of heaven. It could not be regarded as the supreme good in Buddhism. On the other hand, if there did not exist a Land of Purity and Bliss that had adornments, as described in the sūtras, Buddhism would then remain a philosophy [and not a religion].... Every adornment of the Pure Land is nothing more than a manifestation of an ultimate reality that transcends the subject-object dimension.

RYUKYO FUJIMOTO

The provisionally-called 'person' of this defiled world and the provisionally-called 'person' of the Pure Land cannot be definitely called the same or definitely called different.... The reason is that if they were one and the same, then there would be no causality; if they were different, there would be no continuity.

T'AN-LUAN

There is a light unique to night time. The bright light of daytime prevents us from seeing the true self; the shining of the light enables us to move and act in accordance with our knowledge and skill. What enables us to gaze upon the truth of our selves—our lonely, unreliable selves—is the light of the night, like the stars and moon. Not only that, the vastness of the universe cannot be sensed in the daylight; the origins of astronomy can only be found in the evening light. A poet said that moonlight reminded him of the other world. The Pure Land teaching enables us to see the side on which our life is based, the side we do not usually see in our everyday lives.

DAIEI KANEKO

The symbolism of the Pure Land ... would not be possible in Buddhism if it was not reconcilable with the intrinsic nature of Nirvāna or, in other words, if it did not describe in manifested, 'exteriorised' and 'diversified' mode, the ineffable reality of the Self.

FRITHJOF SCHUON

For those for whom there is no Pure Land to go to in the afterlife, it is lonely . . . fearsomely lonely.

ASAHARA SAICHI

The 'Realm of Bliss' is that Pure Land of happiness where there are always countless joys and never any suffering mingled with them.

SHINRAN

Compassion

The Buddha does not always appear as a Buddha. Sometimes he appears as an incarnation of evil, sometimes as a woman, a god, a king or a statesman; sometimes he appears in a brothel or in a gambling house.

In an epidemic, he appears as a healing physician and, in war, he preaches forbearance and mercy for the suffering people; for those who believe that things are everlasting, he preaches transiency and uncertainty; for those who are proud and egoistic, he preaches humility and self-sacrifice; for those who are entangled in the web of worldly pleasures, he reveals the misery of the world.

"Your suffering is my suffering and your happiness is my happiness," said the Buddha and, just as a mother always loves her child, he does not forget that spirit even for a single moment, for it is the nature of Buddhahood to be compassionate.

The Buddha's spirit of compassion is stimulated according to our needs; faith is the reaction to this spirit, and it leads us to Enlightenment, just as a mother realises her motherhood by loving her child; then the child, reacting to that love, feels safe and at ease.

Do not think that the compassion of the Buddha is only for the present life; it is a manifestation of the timeless compassion of the eternal Buddha that has been operative since unknown time, when mankind went astray due to ignorance.

The working of Buddhahood is as everlasting as human ignorance is endless; and, as the depth of ignorance is bottomless, so the Buddha's compassion is boundless.

Thus, the Buddha's compassion embraces all people and his constant consideration is for their happiness. He loves people as parents love their children and he wishes the highest blessedness for them; namely, that they will be able to pass beyond this ocean of life and death.

Just as rain falls on all vegetation, so the Buddha's compassion extends equally to all people. Just as different plants receive particular benefits from the same rain, so people of different natures and circumstances are blessed in different ways.

The world is like a burning house that is forever being destroyed and rebuilt. People, being confused by the darkness of their ignorance, lose their minds in anger, displeasure, jealousy, prejudice and worldly passion. They are like babies in need of a mother; everyone must be dependent upon the Buddha's mercy and compassion.

The Buddha uses all devices to emancipate those who are ready for emancipation. Like a fire that, once kindled, never dies until the fuel is exhausted, so the compassion of the Buddha will never falter until all worldly passions are exhausted. Just as the wind blows away the dust, so the compassion of the Buddha blows away the dust of human suffering.

The moon appears everywhere, over a crowded city, a sleepy village, a mountain, a river. It is seen in the depths of a pond, in a jug of water, in a drop of dew hanging on a leaf. If a man walks hundreds of miles, the moon goes with him. To us, the moon seems to change but the moon does not change. The Buddha is like the moon in following the people of this world in all their changing circumstances, manifesting various appearances; but, in his essence, he does not change.

The Teaching of Buddha

Faith

Faith implies . . . a serene opening up of the depths of one's being to the Buddha's influence.

HAROLD STEWART

Faith is the guide, mother, originator, protector, increaser of virtues, dispeller of doubts, rescuer from the flood of rebirths. Faith is the signpost to the secure city [of the Buddha's realm].

ŚĀNTIDEVA

Faith has a special connotation in religion. It differs from scientific knowledge: when we have the latter, it does not give us any final sense of gratification and happiness; our curiosity is no doubt satisfied, the spirit of inquiry is set at peace but the soul has no feeling of sufficiency or fulfillment.

GESSHŌ SASAKI

When one's faith is firmly established once and for all in everyday life, the Buddha assures us that there will be no danger of losing it; even if we die assailed by fear, anger and other uncomfortable feelings. The Buddha-ego replaces the human ego when we have awakened to the life of faith. Whatever disturbances may take place on the surface of our consciousness, they are like the waves of the ocean whose depth remains forever calm and serene.

SHŪGAKU YAMABE

Faith varies so long as it is based on self-power; for we all have different intellectual capacities and the faith based upon them cannot be identical: whereas the faith based on a power other than the self is one that is given by the Buddha to us, ignorant beings, regardless of our moral attainments. . . . If this faith is understood as 'true mind', it cannot be the deluded heart of the ignorant. It is entirely the Buddha-mind and, when this Buddha-mind is transferred to the heart of the ignorant, it is called *faith*.

KAKUNYO

The Unhindered Path

The logic of faith in Shin Buddhism negates both our efforts to co-operate with, or to add to, Amida's salvation.... Hear the noble teaching of Compassion and Wisdom; then the dark and hard mass of the ego will be crushed of itself.

RYUKYO FUJIMOTO

It is difficult to uncover and recover one's Buddha-nature. It is difficult also to maintain a pure mind in the constant rise and fall of greed, anger and worldly passion; yet faith enables one to do it.

The Teaching of Buddha

The doctrine of salvation by faith teaches that we are saved just as we are. In this doctrine, therefore, no change in the manner of living is required to attain the highest truth. How human is this doctrine!

Synopsis of the Jōdo Shinshū Creed

We often imagine that the ancient lay-disciples took refuge in the Buddha as a mortal being but, in fact, their object of faith was not the corporeal Buddha who entered Nirvāna at the age of eighty but the Dharmakāya, serenely abiding outside the reach of death. If otherwise, the faith of the householders would have been merely an affair of short duration and would not have had such a force as to revolutionise their whole system of thought. That the Dharma is an eternal truth hardly requires to be said.

SHŪGAKU YAMABE

Shinran rejoiced, forgetting himself, in a faith transferred by Amida Buddha's true mind and—instantly taking refuge in the Name in which all necessary practices for our rebirth are perfected—he recited it with a vital force, while constantly harbouring his inner faith, and was thus benefited to his life's end by the Light that transcends time and space.

KAKUNYO

Faith gives us the wisdom to recognise the transiency of life and the grace not to be surprised or grieved at whatever comes to us or with the passing of life itself, knowing that, however conditions and appearances may change, the truth of life always remains unchanged.

Teaching of Buddha

Taking refuge in the Buddha is an act of selfless Faith. It is selfless because it has been given over to us by Amida ... and is, in essence, *Sūnyatā*.

RYUKYO FUJIMOTO

Faith is called the 'seed' without which the plant of spiritual insight cannot start growing. As a matter of fact, those who lack faith can do nothing worthwhile at all. And this faith is much more than the mere acceptance of beliefs.

EDWARD CONZE

Constantly dredge the channel of faith and let the water of Amida's Dharma flow freely.

RENNYO

There are many who think that matters regarding the afterlife, or the Pure Land, have nothing to do with the present life. But when we think of the Buddha showering his great compassion on us who are wandering aimlessly in this world, we come to acknowledge that this faith we thought useless, has become pure salvation and the greatest power in our lives.

KŌSHŌ ŌTANI

In the closed mind of the sceptic, faith is confused with belief, such as his own doctrinaire and emotionally-charged commitment to the groundless opinion that human reason alone is capable of comprehending and explaining everything in the universe (anything that it cannot grasp being conveniently ignored). ... Doubt cannot confer Enlightenment. One of the grave disadvantages of doubt is that it can harden the heart, hindering a free flow of Compassion; another, that it may imprison the mind within the false Void of absence and annihilation.

HAROLD STEWART

The Unhindered Path

Mercy is none other than the nirvanic beatitude which, refracting itself, has fallen into the 'existent nothingness' which is the world. The saving descent of mercy into the soul depends on our faith, which in turn depends on our distress, or rather on the degree to which we are aware of it. Our faith, or our trust, thus derives from two sources; the 'lower' one consists of our incapacity to save ourselves from our wretched state, and the other 'higher' source is the will to save of Amida Buddha.... On the one hand we must acknowledge our inability to save ourselves and, on the other, we must be sure that mercy not only 'can' but 'will' save us in function of our faith. Faith streams forth from the depths of our misery and is nourished by the infinity of Mercy.

FRITHJOF SCHUON

The attainment of Faith in the Sacred Name is to have our entire being radically transformed from its absolute depth. This attainment assures us that we shall never again regress and return to the suffering of the ocean of samsāra.... When we awaken to Eternal Faith, we experience a spiritual tremor that shakes our whole being, so that this new Faith becomes the centre of our spiritual gravity.

RYUKYO FUJIMOTO

What most Western books about Buddhism fail to mention is that none of the spiritual and psycho-physical practices of the Hīnayāna, Mahāyāna or Vajrayāna is going to prove effective if the indispensable prerequisite of Faith is wanting. If we do not take refuge wholeheartedly and without reservations in the Buddha, his doctrine and method, and his order of sages and scholarly teachers, our efforts are likely to be unavailing. We may abide by all the moral precepts and monastic regulations, recite the sūtras and perform the rituals, practise *zazen* and repeat the nembutsu, but, if Faith is lacking, no Deliverance or Enlightenment will result.

But lacking faith or having lost it, how in this faithless age does the earnest seeker go about finding a faith he never owned or regaining one that he has failed to keep? Clearly, Faith cannot be acquired for oneself by any effort of the individual will, for the purpose of the various Buddhist methods is to remove precisely that egoistic obstacle to the reception of Faith. The awakening of ... *shinjin* can no more be self-induced than artistic inspiration can, but must likewise be awaited with a peacefully open heart and mind, and accepted gratefully as a gift from above. Amida is ever prepared to bestow Faith unconditionally on all yet, for most of us, the accumulated consequences of our past stand in the way.

HAROLD STEWART

Men must live in faith and not lead an insignificant life. To live in faith, it is necessary that salvation should come while living an ordinary human existence. It is when we find Light and Life at the hands of Amitābha, and give up our petty plans, that our life in faith begins and becomes significant.

Synopsis of the Jōdo Shinshū Creed

All that is necessary for us is to let the Buddha-mind perform the Buddha's work. *Shinjin*—the Buddha-mind working within us—is, when viewed from our side, a total entrusting to the Primal Vow.

MICHIO TOKUNAGA

Professional incredulity, scepticism as a way of life, is disfavoured by all the scriptures, Buddhist and others alike, because such doubt inhibits the development of the positive spiritual qualities and virtues. What is censured is an ingrained and ungenerous mistrust that disbelieves in everything on principle—except its own cleverness in not being credulous. And yet your hard-headed materialist can become as gullible as the most naïve believer when it comes to accepting as unquestionable truth the latest tentative hypothesis, for he places his faith only in science, which has faith in nothing, not even in itself.

HAROLD STEWART

Nembutsu

The nembutsu which we recite, as well as our faith itself, are the activity of the Buddha. And it is because both are given to us by the Buddha, that they are called faith through the Other-Power.

KŌSHŌ ŌTANI

The spiritual masters of Shin Buddhism always confessed their total lack of any merits and consistently took their refuge solely in the nembutsu. Whatever they may have accomplished in this world, they viewed it as nothing but vainglory.

RYUKYO FUJIMOTO

The teaching and practice for Birth in the Pure Land of Utmost Bliss are our eye and foot in the latter age of this defiled world. Who then—monk or layman, nobleman or commoner—would not depend on it? The practices for attaining enlightenment are, in principle and reality, manifold. For the intelligent and earnest, it is not difficult but, for me, an obstinate and simple man, how is it possible to follow such teachings and such practices? Therefore, I depend on the single gate of the nembutsu.

GENSHIN

The nembutsu is not merely to utter Amida's Name and recollect his Great Compassion. It is the losing of our self-will to the will of Amida. It is coming to our existential limits and jumping over the abyss which opens up before us.

KENRYO KANAMATSU

The Tathāgata's Primal Vow originates in his deep sorrow over the human condition. Therefore, the power manifested in the nembutsu moves us towards the other shore, beyond this world of birth-and-death, and calls on us to reflect upon our inability to detach ourselves from love and hate.

DAIEI KANEKO

Selected Dharma Passages

If Faith is the mental state of accepting Amida Buddha's saving power, then the Name represents the saving activity. In the aspirant, the Name reveals itself through Faith as the nembutsu.

MITSUYUKI ISHIDA

The Nembutsu signifies that very instant in which we and Amida come into contact and become One. However, that 'instant' embodied by the nembutsu subsequently continues on throughout our lives, up to the moment of our death, at which time we enter Amida's realm.

RYUKYO FUJIMOTO

If you were to say that the Primal Vow, or Other-Power, has no connection to 'real life', I would agree completely. However, from the standpoint of a person who does nembutsu, that which we think of as 'real life' is adrift from the very thing it should be rooted in. The life that we call reality, and to which we are clinging, is like rootless trees and grasses, simply afloat in a moving stream, going this way and that.

DAIEI KANEKO

Amida Buddha embraces us in his arms of Compassion because, for him, the sense of separateness and discrimination that is inbred in all of us amounts to nothing but an illusion. . . . Let us then keep the Light of the Holy Name ever burning in the inner sanctuaries of our minds, wherever we go and whatever we are doing. For the Name turns fear into hope, sorrow into consolation and joy, and hate into compassion.

RYUKYO FUJIMOTO

Other-Power

Non-ego is the highest ideal for all Buddhists. The spiritual ancestors of Shin Buddhism regarded Faith in Other-Power as the most practical way of annihilating our illusory attachment to the self.

RYUKYO FUJIMOTO

Attachment to one's own self-power must be discarded and Amida's saving power and boundless mercy must be trusted so that one may attain deliverance from the cycle of delusion, from painstaking but futile effort, and from deeper delusion which entails further pain. In fact, we are so deeply attached to our own selves and so blindly convinced of our own power that we cannot easily give ourselves up to the all-embracing power and compassion of Amida Buddha. Indeed, we may go through several stages in the process of conversion before we attain the Faith of Other-Power. Faith, as such, is simply another name for Amida's Mind of Wisdom and Compassion transferred to the aspirant. . . . Hence, Faith is the cause of Enlightenment. Faith, as it appears in the aspirant's consciousness, is the mental state of doubtlessness, joy, security and gratitude.

MITSUYUKI ISHIDA

The Pure Land masters noted a fundamental flaw in other formulations of Buddhist thought. If we are to gain liberation—the state of no-self—through our own efforts, then how is it possible to attain no-self through self? This is like trying to wash out mud using muddy water. We can only reach no-self through no power of the self.

Jōdo Shinshū: A Guide

In the *jiriki* way of thinking where our ego works, we imagine that we can learn and practise the way of severing ourselves from the bondage of birth-and-death. This inevitably tends to cultivate in us a feeling of pride in self-assertiveness and this, at the same time, tends to assume a contemptuous attitude towards others, because of the learning and discipline we have attained. As long as one stays in this

Selected Dharma Passages

state of mind, there is no spiritual equanimity, which is sought after by all religious souls. This is where jiriki fails.

IPPEN

The assurance, on our part, of being the objects of the Primal Vow is identical with the enlightenment on the part of Amida himself. Such is the idea at the base of the *tariki* doctrine. In this doctrine, the enlightenment attained by oneself, as the Buddhists of former generations understood it, has taken the form of faith in the enlightenment of Amida.

D. T. SUZUKI

Only when the seeker has come to realise the ineffectuality of all his exertions to save himself, only after his egoistic will is committed to self-abandonment with the utmost sincerity, can Amida Buddha come to his aid. Then he bestows his gratuitous blessing of Boundless Light (or Pure Consciousness) that transcends space, and his Endless Life (or Pure Being) that transcends time. Unhindered by interference from the self, the Divine Name filled with Faith will repeat itself spontaneously in the devotee's inmost heart and flood his whole being with its miraculous graces of compassion and wisdom in joy and peace.

It is useless trying to convince, by rational argument, those brought up in the Western tradition who overvalue the individual ego. They must ultimately come to the realisation that, in fact, only Other-Power is the bestower of power on all beings. There is, in truth, no self-power because of the basic Buddhist teaching of *anattā*; non-ego, selflessness (not unselfishness).

When you receive shinjin from Amida, gratitude for the free gift will arise naturally. Such spontaneity cannot be imitated by an individual act of will or by ingenious argument, which always betray their lack of authenticity.

HAROLD STEWART

Beauty

Beauty is like the sun: it acts without detours, without dialectical intermediaries; its ways are free, direct, incalculable; like love, to which it is closely connected, it can heal, unloose, appease, unite or deliver through its simple radiance. The image of the Buddha is like the sound of that celestial music which could charm a rose tree into flowering amid the snow; such was Shakyamuni—for it is said that the buddhas bring salvation not only through their teaching but also through their superhuman beauty—and such is his sacramental image.

He who says peace, says beauty; the image of the Tathāgata . . . shows that beauty, in its root or essence, is compounded of serenity and mercy; formal harmony appeals to us because it bespeaks profound goodness and inexhaustible wealth, appeasement and plenitude.

Like a magnet, the beauty of the Buddha draws all the contradictions of the world and transmutes them into radiant silence; the image deriving therefrom appears as a drop of the dew of immortality fallen into the chilly world of forms and crystallised into a human form, a form accessible to men.

Frithjof Schuon

Jōdo Shinshū

Jōdo Shinshū is not a religion of goodness but a religion of truth. Whoever believes in the truth is saved, whether they are good or bad.

GESSHŌ SASAKI

Buddhism is a great spiritual asset bequeathed to humanity by Shakyamuni, the Enlightened One. But its scope is so large and varied that people today may be at a loss as to how to access this treasure-store of Dharma. We cannot possibly read all the scriptures, or successfully practise the methods of attaining *bodhi*, while busily occupied in earning a living. Besides, our intellect and practice are deceptive and misleading due to the deep-rooted, delusory self-attachment that blinds us spiritually. This impossibility of attaining *bodhi* on our side is made a possibility by Amida Buddha, who channels the way for us to reach the Castle of Enlightenment by turning all the truths and merits of Dharma over to us. Herein lies the essential characteristic of Shin Buddhism.

KENJU MASUYAMA

Since the Primal Vow works for the sake of saving beings with defiled karma, if a person realises its working, he becomes aware of his defiled nature. It is with this realisation that Shinran laments the corruption of Buddhism; not as an outside observer but as one who is involved in it.

MICHIO TOKUNAGA

Amida Buddha and His Pure Land are the manifestations of Thusness, through the Vows, and they are the source of Shin Buddhist teaching and the activity of salvation by which sentient beings attain the same Enlightenment as Amida's. Amida is the Buddha of eternal Life and boundless Light, the embodiment of Wisdom and Compassion. Though presented as the object of worship and reverence, he is, in fact, Truth and Reality in action, capable of dissipating our ignorance and destroying our evil passions. Those who have been led to the Pure Land attain Enlightenment and join in his eternal activity.

MITSUYUKI ISHIDA

The Unhindered Path

It is no exaggeration to say that Shinran's unceasing activities of spreading the Dharma, stern moral life, patience, energy, tireless nembutsu and joy in Amida's *prajñā* might be a pattern of the Buddhist life. They are all the more Buddhistic because they were done unconsciously, out of his disinterested sense of gratitude, and not from a desire to gain birth in the Pure Land.

RYUKYO FUJIMOTO

According to Jōdo Shinshū, religions that only promote this-worldly benefits are considered a false path. But this does not mean that Jōdo Shinshū is a religion that ignores this present life. Rather, by showing us the ground of our actual life, it truly engages with our real living. What we need to understand is the difference between benefits in this life and this-worldly benefits. Worldly benefits are those like escaping calamities and ensuring a long life. Benefits in this life are trans-worldly, like constantly practicing great compassion. While Shinran did not deny that nembutsu followers also enjoy benefits in this world, what he rejoiced in, solely, were the benefits in this life.

DAIEI KANEKO

The Pure Land teaching established by Shinran tells us that we are all embraced by the power of Amida Buddha's Primal Vow. Entrusting in this Vow enables all to live in the present with confidence and peace of mind, and assures us that we will be born in the Pure Land where we will attain Enlightenment. The purpose of this teaching is to enable all to live our lives to the fullest, becoming aware of both the potential and the limitations of this world.

Jōdo Shinshū: A Guide

Among the many varieties of Buddhism, the Pure Land teaching most deserves the epithet 'other-worldly', often erroneously applied to Buddhism as a whole. Pure Land doctrine teaches that this world is an arena of unavoidable suffering and frustration, and holds out the vivid prospect of rebirth in another, better world, where sickness, pain and death do not exist. This world is a hopeless trap, from which we can escape only by the power of Amitābha. Unless we

234

attain rebirth in the Pure Land, peace and happiness, to say nothing of enlightenment, are beyond reach.

J.C. CLEARY

Shin Buddhism is said to be a religion of hearing: *sravana*. It is categorically true that neither our own practice nor our own thinking assures our rebirth into the Land of Purity. However, 'hearing the Sacred Name' is identified with faith which is the cause of our rebirth.

RYUKYO FUJIMOTO

Other Buddhist schools emphasise that the truth is to be seen and realised. But Shinran, knowing that to be impossible, knowing that humans can never detach themselves from a life of anxiety and suffering, caused by blind passions, entered into the dharma of hearing and contemplation. This is the uniqueness of Shin Buddhism.

DAIEI KANEKO

There is more truth or reality in a world of values than in that of actualities, and the flower of faith blooms and bears fruit in the former rather than the latter, for a world of facts is a limited one, bound in time and space where the highest imagination feels so constrained. The absolute faith Jōdo Shinshū teaches transcends such limitations and, naturally, is not to be sought for in a world of relativities.

GESSHŌ SASAKI

True liberation must be that which gives us the strength to continue, even if things do not go as we wish, fully recognising that all problems are transient in nature. In this way, we can transcend any obstacle and live life to the utmost. The Jōdo Shinshū teaching explains that such strength comes from Amida Buddha's ceaseless work to bring about our liberation, and to have us experience the benevolence of his Vow-Power, which will ultimately bring about our birth in the Pure Land. It is what sustains us spiritually and gives us lifelong fortitude. Choosing to proceed along this path will lead us to attain the same awakening as the Buddha.

Jōdo Shinshū: A Guide

The Unhindered Path

The doctrine of Shinran provides a wonderful synthesis between the devotional and the sapiential paths: to start with, it envisages the 'Pure Land', the *Sukhāvatī* paradise, in its aspect of transcendence, hence of identity with Nirvāna; similarly, it reminds us that by virtue of universal analogies, death can serve to rend the veil of illusion, and hence can be an occasion for illumination and deliverance.

FRITHJOF SCHUON

Some may think that Shin Buddhism is immoral or anti-ethical and, therefore, has nothing to do with our everyday life. But, in point of fact, Shin has a very keen critical sense of our moral imperfections and teaches that, because of these, we ought to be humble, penitent and grateful.

GESSHŌ SASAKI

It might very well be true that there is no life, either before or after, this life. But if so, this life would become a floating one, with nothing to rely on. Nembutsu followers sense both the next life and the lives before this one. The Buddha's world must be an eternal one that transcends past, present and future. It is just like the sun, which does not distinguish between the night and day experienced on earth. But ordinary, unenlightened beings can anticipate entering the eternal world after this life.

DAIEI KANEKO

We live by reason, though it is imperfect. Yet any attempt, based on reason, to sanctify our lives will fail, no matter how hard we try. Only when we are led by the power of Amida, and by aspiration for rebirth in his Pure Land, can we conquer this life. It does not matter how bad our karma is; it does not matter how imperfect our reason is. The power of Amida purifies us and converts our evil passions into virtues. In what we may call faith, we are given his power. And, at the same time, a pure, real, serene and eternal life will be infused into our own life which had been miserable, false, finite and unreal. This true life will be constructed upon a framework of faith which becomes, not only the invisible foundation of our life, but also an inner power which enables us to realise purification beyond the realm of ethics. This awakening results in our reciting the nembutsu in complete thankfulness and in happiness. This is the very essence of the teaching of Shinran, a teaching he realised only after a desperate spiritual struggle.

KŌSHŌ ŌTANI

References to Appendix

The quotations in this appendix are drawn from the following sources and have, where appropriate, been slightly adapted for clarity and consistency. They have also been rendered into British English in keeping with the style observed in the rest of this work.

Shōshin Ge: The Gātha of True Faith in the Nembutsu (Kyoto: Ryūkoku University, 1961).

The Jōdo Wasan (Kyoto: Ryūkoku University, 1965).

The Kōsō Wasan (Kyoto: Ryūkoku University, 1974).

The Shōzōmatsu Wasan (Kyoto: Ryūkoku University, 1980).

Collected Works of Shinran (Kyoto: Jōdo Shinshū Hongwanji-ha, 1997).

Principal Teachings of the True Sect of Pure Land (Kyoto: Ōtani-ha Hongwanji, 1915).

Synopsis of the Jōdo Shinshū Creed (Kyoto: Educational Department of the West Hongwanji, 1922).

Buddhism and Jōdo Shinshū (San Francisco: Buddhist Churches of America, 1955).

Shinshū Seiten: Jōdo Shin Buddhist Teaching (San Francisco: Buddhist Churches of America, 1978).

The Teaching of Buddha (Tokyo: Bukkyō Dendō Kyōkai, 1986).

Jōdo Shinshū: A Guide (Kyoto: Jōdo Shinshū Hongwanji-ha, 2002).

CLEARY, J.C. (tr.), *Pure Land, Pure Mind: The Buddhism of Masters Chu-hung and Tsung-pen* (New York: Sūtra Translation Committee of the United States and Canada, 1994).

CONZE, Edward (ed.), *Buddhist Scriptures* (London: Penguin, 1959).

CONZE, Edward, *Buddhism: Its Essence and Development* (New York: Harper & Row, 1959).

Selected Dharma Passages

—————. *Buddhist Thought in India* (Ann Arbor: University of Michigan Press, 1967).

—————. *Thirty Years of Buddhist Studies* (Oxford: Bruno Cassirer, 1967).

COOMARASWAMY, Ananda, *Hinduism and Buddhism* (New Delhi: Munshiram Manoharlal, 1986).

FUJIKI, Terumi, *Myōkōnin Genza-san* [Vol. I] (Anaheim: Buddhist Education Center, 2008).

—————. *Myōkōnin Genza-san* [Vol. II] (Anaheim: Buddhist Education Center, 2008).

FUJIMOTO, Ryukyo, *An Outline of the Triple Sūtra of Shin Buddhism* [Vol. I] (Kyoto: Honpa Hongwanji Press, 1955).

—————. *An Outline of the Triple Sūtra of Shin Buddhism* [Vol. II] (Kyoto: Hyyaka-en Press, 1960).

—————. *The Tannishō* (Kyoto: Honpa Hongwanji Press, 1955).

GRIMM, George, *The Doctrine of the Buddha* (Berlin: Akademie-Verlag, 1958).

—————. *Buddhist Wisdom: The Mystery of the Self* (Delhi: Motilal Banarsidass, 1978).

—————. *Perennial Questions: The Fundamental Religious Problems and their Solution in Indian Thought* (Delhi: Motilal Banarsidass, 1979).

HAKEDA, Yoshito (tr.), *The Awakening of Faith in the Mahāyāna* (New York: Columbia University Press, 1967).

HEARN, Lafcadio, *The Buddhist Writings of Lafcadio Hearn* (London: Wildwood House, 1981).

KAKEHASHI, Jitsuen, *The Shin Buddhist View of Birth-and-Death* (San Francisco: Buddhist Churches of America, 2000).

KANAMATSU, Kenryo, *Naturalness* (Los Angeles: The White Path Society, 1956).

KANEKO, Daiei, 'On the *Kyōgyōshinshō*', *The Pure Land: Journal of the*

International Association of Shin Buddhist Studies, New Series No. 26, (2010–2011), pp. 114–134.

KIYOZAWA, Manshi, *December Fan* (Kyoto: Higashi Hongwanji, 1984).

LA ROCHEFOUCAULD, François, *Maxims* (London: Penguin, 1959).

McGOVERN, William Montgomery, *An Introduction to Mahāyāna Buddhism* (London: Kegan Paul, Trench, Trubner & Co., 1922).

ŌTANI, Kōshō, *Sermons on Shin Buddhism* (Kyoto: Honpa Hongwanji Press, 1957).

PALLIS, Marco, *The Way and the Mountain* (Bloomington: World Wisdom, 2008).

PYE, Michael (ed.), *Beyond Meditation: Expressions of Japanese Shin Buddhist Spirituality* (London: Equinox, 2011).

SAHER, P. J., *Happiness and Immortality: George Grimm's Investigations into the Secrets of Buddhism* (London: George Allen and Unwin, 1970).

SASAKI, Gesshō, *A Study of Shin Buddhism* (Kyoto: The Eastern Buddhist Society, 1925).

SCHUMANN, Hans Wolfgang, *Buddhism: An Outline of its Teachings and Schools* (London: Rider & Co., 1973).

SCHUON, Frithjof, *Treasures of Buddhism* (Bloomington: World Wisdom, 1993).

STEWART, Harold, *By the Old Walls of Kyoto: A Year's Cycle of Landscape Poems with Prose Commentaries* (New York: Weatherhill, 1981).

SUZUKI, Beatrice Lane, *Impressions of Mahāyāna Buddhism* (London: Luzac & Co., 1940).

SUZUKI, Daisetz Teitaro, *On Indian Mahāyāna Buddhism* (New York: Harper & Row, 1968).

————. 'The Development of the Pure Land Doctrine in Buddhism', *The Eastern Buddhist,* Vol. 3, No. 4 (1925), pp. 285–326.

UTSUKI, Nishu, *The Shin Sect: A School of Mahāyāna Buddhism* (Kyoto: Hompa Honganji, 1937).

The author is a Shin Buddhist priest from Australia. He was ordained in 1994 at the Temple of the Primal Vow (Hongan-ji) in Kyoto and has published a number of works including *Call of the Infinite* and *The Fragrance of Light*.

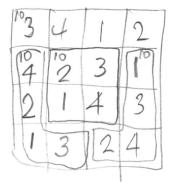

Printed in Great Britain
by Amazon